THE SPIRITS OF OUIJA
Four Decades of Communication

Karen A. Dahlman

THE SPIRITS OF OUIJA
Four Decades of Communication

Copyright © 2013 by Creative Visions Publications

FIRST EDITION

Published by Creative Visions Publications
PO Box 1496
San Clemente, CA 92674
United States of America
creativevisionspublications.com

Publish Date: October 2013
ISBN: 978-0615898674

Photography & Cover Design by Karen A. Dahlman

ALL RIGHTS RESERVED
No portion of this book can be reproduced without the express written permission of Creative Visions Publications.

The intent of the author is only to offer information of a general nature to you in your quest for emotional and spiritual well-being. In the event you use any of the information in this book for yourself, which is your constitutional right, the author and the publisher assume no responsibility for your actions.

OUIJA® and MYSTIFYING ORACLE® are trademarks of Hasbro, Inc.
The Hasko Mystic Tray®, the Hasko Mystic Board® and the Mystic Hand® are trademarks of Haskelite Mfg. Corp.
SWAMI MYSTERY TALKING BOARD® is a trademark of Gift Craft Co.
HeartMath® is a trademark of HeartMath, LLC.

The use of these trademarks within this publication was not authorized by, nor is this publication sponsored by or associated with the trademark owners.

Author's Note

Some names and identifying details within this book have been changed to protect the privacy of individuals. Any changed name that may share a resemblance to a known person is by sheer coincidence.

The pronouns she and he are used alternately to indicate the third-person singular and to make the reading relative for both sexes. Also, I shift between using the first, second and third-person pronouns to direct the message to you, the reader, or to us, in a collective sense.

I use the words "entities" and "spirits" interchangeably when speaking in general terms, because not only have I spoken with deceased beings, but also with consciousness that is alive, such as Higher Selves and animals.

When you see an asterisk following a word, you can find that word listed in the Glossary Section at the back of the book, defined as the author intended.

Dedication

HAPPINESS LIES IN THE PATH NOT THE DESTINATION
- *The Higher Self*

This book is dedicated to all of you who aspire to live your unlimited possibilities. The words imparted on the following pages are dedicated to you. I am thrilled that you are embarking upon your path of discovery of the treasures found within. Just remember, it is during the travels along your path that the greatest of joys are experienced and the deepest of possibilities are found!

Acknowledgments

THE SOUL IS ALL THERE IS
- *The Sun*

I wish to express my heartfelt thanks and gratitude to everyone who assisted me along my path of learning to communicate with the Great Beyond. There have been many helpers over the past forty years and to each I appreciate your enthusiasm you shared with me for my tool, the Ouija Board. Without mentioning your names, you know who you are!

Thank you Mom and Dad for working it out with Santa Claus so I received my first Ouija Board for Christmas, thus starting me on this enlightening, forty-year journey. Also, many thanks to the following people, Chris G., Brian B., Roberta L., Rhonda W., Elise S., Victoria V. and Bev M. for sharing your Ouija experiences within this book and allowing all to see a snapshot into your life. A special thank you to my editor, Paulina Patsek, who not only edited this book, but also edited my first book, *The Spirit of Creativity: Embodying Your Soul's Passion*, many, many years ago. I appreciate her loyal dedication and comprehensive grasp of the topics of which I write. And last but not least, a big thank you to my spirit friends who chose the path of helping me and many others to endeavor to find our own internal truths, while illuminating our way back home to source.

Table of Contents

Author's Note iii

Dedication iv

Acknowledgments v

Introduction 1

Chapter 1 - Ouija History 6

  History of Ouija 6

    Founders of the Talking Board 9

    How Ouija got its name 12

    Ouija & Talking Board Expert 14

  Spiritualism & Divination 15

Chapter 2 - Misconceptions: Jeer & Fear 20

  The Bad Rap 20

    Hasbro & Hollywood 24

  Fear 27

    Platonic & Neo-Platonic Philosophy 28

    Theurgy & Sciomancy 29

  Nothing New Under the Sun 30

    Get the Drift? 31

Chapter 3 - My History with Ouija **34**

   The Whammy! 36

   Eye-Opening 38

   Out of the Closet 39

   Ouija Goes to College 42

Chapter 4 - The Proper Use **49**

   My Turning Point 49

      Uh Oh; Now What? 54

   Session Preparation 56

      The Internal Space 57

      The External Space 59

   The Ambiance - Bringing it All Together 62

      Schedule the Session 62

      Elevate Your Senses 63

      Breathe to Ground & Open Yourself 64

      Respect for Yourself & the Spirits 65

      Opening the Portal 66

      Closing the Portal 66

      Patience with the Process 67

     Hips to Heart Breathing 69

     Opening Protective Prayer 71

Atmospheric & Planetary Effects on a Session 73

Your Spiritual Practice...78

Chapter 5 - Going Public...82

Coming out of the Closet..82

And Into the Light...85

Chapter 6 - The Deceased 90

Spirits & Ghosts...90

Spirits...92

Wilma Jean 93

Very Important!...97

Ghosts & Spirit Releasement 101

Samuel..102

Very Important!...104

Tom McEachrun...106

Hector..108

Theresa & Styrmy 110

Spirits Becoming Earthbound Ghosts..118

Anne King 118

Sharon, Jay & Steven 122

Chapter 7 - Angels, Guides & Ethereal Beings.......................126

Mary Angel..126

The Sun & the Moon..129

Other Spirit Guides 134

Chapter 8 - Consciousness Communication.........136

The Higher Self..137

Higher Self Messages 139

Self Love & Heart...139

Knowledge & Truth..140

Believe & Know..142

The Soul..143

Problems are Opportunities.....................................144

Dreams 145

Talents 145

Happiness..146

Change 146

Money..147

Animal Communication 147

Chapter 9 - Beyond Messages: Teaching & Lessons 165

Spirits' Teachings & What I Learned 165

The Sill 165

Heart & Soul 167

Inside...168

Limitations 169

Change 170

Money 171

Flow 174

Dreams 175

What Others Learned **177**

Chris G. 177

Brian B. 179

Roberta L. 180

Rhonda W. 182

Elise S. 182

Victoria V. 185

Bev M. 186

Glossary **188**

Bibliography **190**

About the Author **193**

Previous Work 195

Author Contact 196

Introduction

You ask me why I wrote this book? Quite simply put, I wrote this book to share with you my path, just a path into our endless possibilities for life. Although, it is not a politically correct path to forge, it has been an incredible, eye-opening, heart-expanding and mind-blowing path for me over the past forty years and that is all that matters.

I say, "Create for yourself the best journey and open yourself to spiritual truths along the way!" Everyone must find their own path as they traverse through life and learn about themselves in relationship to life. After all, I believe that life is our chance to express exactly what our souls came here to express and that would be your greatest gifts to share, your talents!

We are only blocked by fear, which cripples us. We are skyrocketed ahead by love, which expands us. You get to choose. That's the coolest part about this path. You have all the power to choose. It's liberating to find out that life never ends as you may think, when a person dies. The deceased never leave us. You are never alone. You have many, many supporters in the Great Beyond*, cheering you on every single time you feel love in your heart, for they know that this love-feeling is what will open you to your Greatest Self*.

The Spirits come to teach you about your soul and its mission within your life. They want nothing more than for you to express your greatest gifts, talents and feelings. They believe in the myriad of emotions and want you to come to know yourself by facing these emotions and learning to love yourself no matter what you see and feel. They offer great insights, nudging you to look within, as they know that all of your answers are inside. They teach you how to do this within yourself in a loving manner, so that you may endeavor to merge with that all-knowing part within you.

Our spirit guides, our angels, our guardian spirits are awaiting your contact. Some of you are already in contact and those of you who are not, this is just one path, one way, in which to do this. I most definitely invite you to join me on the following pages as I share my story, my adventures and the knowledge gleaned and lessons learned from out of my experiences with the Ouija Board.

I present to you my odyssey, which began back in 1973 and continues into present time. All that you will be reading on the following pages has been tediously saved within many, many notebooks filled with the messages received from my spirit friends since 1989. The sessions that happened before 1989 are recounted from memory and from personal journals I kept in parallel throughout the years. Their messages are timeless. As I reference my notebooks and their teachings, I find myself reliving that specific session within that moment in time, once again, reminding me that life is special and grand.

This book is written in a format that allows you to jump around from section to section if you prefer and go right to the stories. However, I highly recommend that you do not start your own personal experiences with a Talking Board or Ouija Board until you read Chapter 4 in its entirety. In this chapter I provide the most pertinent and relevant factors to implement when attempting your own sessions. It is so important to me that you only have positive experiences from your sessions. I will stress this again; you must read this section first!

With this being said, the book was also written in a sequential manner to introduce the history of Ouija from its days of patenting, obtaining its name, to its rise in popularity and to its fall from grace. You'll get a glimpse into my history with the Board and how to use it correctly, for beneficial and positive means, such as spiritual development and discovering your talents. The Ouija Board's history is huge, as it spans the echoes of time, all the while, remaining one of America's most controversial, yet most famous pop icons of today. Come learn why.

So, without further adieu, I invite you to turn the page and step behind the veil of the unseen and meet my spirit friends, up close and personal. A whole new world is awaiting you. Are you ready to claim your world?

Copy of the original Ouija Board patent by Elijah Bond, granted in 1891.

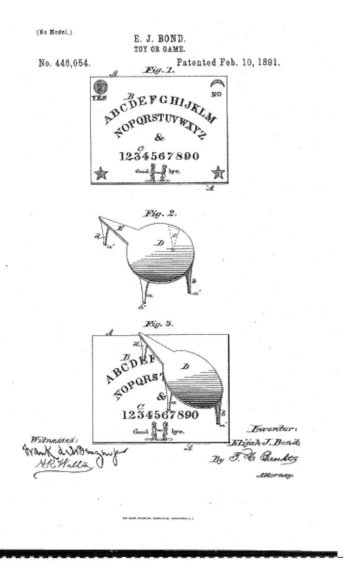

Chapter 1 - Ouija History

TELEPATHY, SPIRIT VOICE? SUBCONSCIOUS MIND?
WHICH SPEAKS THROUGH THE MYSTIC OUIJA BOARD?
-Search Magazine Advertisement, December 1957

History of Ouija

The year was 1890 and the date was the twenty-eight of May, when attorney Elijah Jefferson Bond filed a United States patent for the Ouija Board. Two city businessmen, Charles Wesley Kennard and William Henry Ashton Maupin, were listed as its assignees. On the tenth of February 1891 the registered patent was granted, thus giving birth to the "Ouija or Egyptian luck-Board," as the patent listed it.

In 1891, Bond was a busy businessman, as he was granted a Canadian patent for the Ouija Board one month to the day from the United States patent. The International Novelty Company struck a deal with Bond and obtained the rights to his Canadian Patent. The International Novelty Company in turn, worked a deal with Canadian company, Copp Clark Company Limited, to lease the rights to manufacture the Ouija Board for sale in Canada. This lease was in place until 1904 when a fire destroyed their entire Ouija Board inventory. In 1908, the Copp Clark Company re-manufactured the Ouija Board and then held their own patent and royalties from the Board, since the original patent had expired in 1901. It was only good for ten years. Meanwhile, in the United States, eighteen days after Kennard and Maupin were listed as the Ouija patents assignees, they sold their rights to the Kennard Novelty Company. Having incorporated as a company several months earlier in October of 1890, Kennard and Maupin were listed as two of the owners along with three other businessmen. In early February of 1891 the Kennard Novelty Company obtained the Ouija trademark and into business the company went, producing Ouija Boards for just shy of two years. Two owners of the company, Colonel Washington Bowie III, who fronted a majority of the capital for the company, along with Harry Welles Rusk, reorganized the company by removing the other men from it.

When they reorganized, they moved the company to another location in Baltimore and hired William Fuld to run its operation, who had originally worked as a varnisher at the Kennard Novelty Company. At this time, the company name was changed to the Ouija Novelty Company. Over the years, Fuld filed numerous patents and trademarks that made the Ouija Board better and looking more like the Ouija Board we know today. Reputedly, he holds the most patents and trademarks surrounding the Ouija.

By 1898, Bowie and Rusk were personally assigned all assets of the Ouija Novelty Company they owned, resulting in the majority going to Bowie. Within months of doing so, they struck a three-year deal with Fuld and his brother Isaac to produce Ouija Boards while Bowie and Rusk earned royalties.

Three years later, in the summer of 1901, when the contract expired, Bowie and Rusk exclusively signed on with brother William to manufacture the Ouija Board. After a fallout with his brother Isaac, Fuld launched his own company in his namesake, the William Fuld Manufacturing Company, and began producing the Boards for Bowie and Rusk. However, Rusk left the partnership after selling his stake in the Ouija Novelty Company to Bowie for one hundred dollars and Bowie solely began to collect all contract royalties from the Ouija Board sales until 1919. April of that year, Bowie stepped aside from Ouija and assigned all of its assets, rights and interests to Fuld.

On the twenty fourth of February 1927, Fuld died from his heart being pierced by a broken rib after falling from his factory's three-story roof. His children took over his business and ran it until it was sold in February 1966 to Parker Brothers, exactly 39 years from the date of Fuld's death.

Founders of the Talking Board

Even before the patent was filed for the Ouija Board and its accompanying planchette and before other talking Boards were created and being used, there are varying opinions to who and when the first talking board was invented. What constitutes a Talking Board? A Talking Board is comprised of a detachable, free-moving message indicator on which the fingers rest and a surface in which the alphabet is written on it. Now, just taking your finger off the planchette and try putting your finger on exactly who originally created the talking Board and varying accounts and stories will surface. In this section I've included five compelling accounts backed by written and dated correspondence, discussing the invention and use of this divination tool*.

Reported in an article published in the *Quarterly Review*, October of 1871, was an eye-witness account of two women who used a planchette that moved under their hands while pointing to successive letters and images on a card, while seemingly receiving spelled communication.

In December of 1876, an individual with the byname *LK* shared within the *American Spiritualist Magazine* that he and his wife had developed a new method for communication with the spirits. He explained that he painted a table with the letters of the alphabet on it and they employed the use of a rounded and polished rod that was wider and rougher on the topside. They rested their fingers on the topside to avoid slipping off as the rod moved over the table, pointing to letter after letter, spelling out the messages received. He offered to share this new method with the magazine's readers.

The New York Tribune released an article entitled: *The New Planchette: A Mysterious Talking Board and Table Over Which Northern Ohio Is Agitated* in March of 1886. The article shared a man's account of what he had witnessed in Ohio and what he further explained was a new, yet mysterious form of communication that involved a little table and a Board. He shared how the Board was inscribed with the alphabet, including "yes" and the "no" and two other salutations, "good-evening" and "good-night." He explained that two people placed the Board upon their shared laps and gripped the two corners of the little table closest to them with their forefingers and thumb as the little table rested on the larger Board beneath it. They asked questions as the little table moved over the letters, to rest its legs on a specific letter and spell out the answers to their questions.

Nearly the same time in 1886, but only a few months later in June of 1886, the *Boston Globe* describes a similar device called "The Witch Board" that had a strikingly similar appearance and mannerism to working it. However, the salutations included: "Good-by" and "Good-

10

day," in addition to the "yes" and the "no" located in the four corners of the Board. It was developed and sold by the nation's largest toy manufacturer at the time, W. S. Reed Toy Company.

Fascinatingly, the treasurer of the Reed Toy Company sent President Grover Cleveland a Witch Board as a wedding present when he married his wife who was twenty-seven years his junior. The wedding also happened in June of 1886.

Another Ouija Board founder's story, with the most controversy surrounding it and only because the documentation to fully support it has not been discovered, is about Ernest Charles Reiche, a cabinetmaker. This story takes place in 1886 and links Earnest Charles Reiche with Charles Wesley Kennard. One version of the story explains that Reiche developed a Board with the alphabet and "yes" and the "no" placed on it and used a writing planchette, which was retrofitted after he removed the pencil leg and replaced it with only pegged legs. This planchette moved around the Board, pointing to the letters while resting on his lap. The story continued that Reiche sold the Board to his friend, Kennard, who in turn founded the Kennard Novelty Company and began developing the Board and selling it.

Now, the other version of this story is a flipped rendition, having Kennard as the inventor of the Ouija Board. There were reportedly a series of letters to the *Boston Globe* in 1920 with Kennard explaining the he alone is the original inventor of the Ouija Board. He claimed that he laid a breadboard on his lap with penciled letters and numbers on it, while either a saucer or a small table (two different accounts) under his fingers glided across the Board. Kennard approached the cabinetmaker, Reiche, and requested him to make several devices of this prototype. When Reiche was unable to take on any more additional work, Kennard turned towards Bond, whom he just met, for assistance with the manufacturing of the Board. Supposedly, that's when Bond being an attorney, filed the original Ouija patent, incorporating improvements to its design and then, signed over its rights to Kennard and Maupin.

How Ouija got its name

Of course, there are varying accounts to how Ouija received its name. The account with Reiche at the helm of its invention is one of the versions. In this story it's believed that Reiche named the Board "Ouija" because during a session, the Board told him that it meant "luck" in Egyptian. Could this be why it was named "Ouija or Egyptian luck-Boards" in the original patent granted to Bond in 1891?

Very similarly, another story tells of Kennard discovering the name of the Board during a session. This session was held with Bond's sister-in-law, Miss Peters being present. Kennard stated,

"I remarked that we had not yet settled upon a name, and as the Board had helped us in other ways, we would ask it to propose one. It spelled out O-U-I-J-A. When I asked the meaning of the word it said 'Good Luck.' Miss Peters there upon drew upon her neck a chain, which had at the end a locket, on it a figure of a woman and at the top the word 'Ouija'. We asked her if she had thought of the name, and she said she had not. We then adopted the word. There were present Mr. Bond, his wife, his son, Miss Peters and myself."

As the story continues, immediately following that exciting session, a press release posted in the Baltimore Sun on December 6, 1890.

"The Ouija"

THE WONDER OF THE NINETEENTH CENTURY

This most interesting and mysterious Talking Board has awakened great curiosity wherever shown. It surpasses in its results second sight, mind reading or clairvoyance. It consists of a small table placed upon a large Board containing the alphabet and numerals. By simply resting the fingers of two persons upon the small table, it moves, and to all intents and purposes becomes a living sensible thing giving intelligent answers to any questions that can be propounded. Wonderful as this may seem, the "Ouija" was thoroughly tested and the above facts demonstrated at the United States patent office before the

13

patent was allowed. For sale by all first-class Toy Dealers and Stationers. Manufactured by The Kennard Novelty Company, 220 South Charles Street, Baltimore, Md.

Ouija & Talking Board Expert

Robert L. Murch, Jr., the owner of Williamfuld.com, is the world's foremost expert on the history of the Ouija Board. Not only is he a noted historian, he is an avid collector of Ouija and other Talking Boards, which began in 1993 with his first purchased antique Ouija Board. His current collection now boasts three hundred Talking Boards. In 2007 he launched the williamfuld.com website that publicly shares his comprehensive research and fantastic collection of Boards.

Often consulted by historical societies, museums, Hollywood studios, paranormal groups, the press and toy companies, to name a few, Robert's goal is to preserve Ouija's legacy and provide its accurate history. I highly recommend you check out his thorough website to learn more about the Ouija Board's history. It not only contains the inventors' and manufacturers' history but also has an interesting display of customer letters, article reprints and advertisement copy about the Board from its inception until it was sold to Parker Brothers in 1966.

Spiritualism & Divination

The religious movement known as Spiritualism believes that the human soul* continues to exist after death and engages in the practice of speaking with the deceased. It was mainly a movement of mid and upper class participants, especially popular amongst the women, cropped up in America around the mid 1800s and grew in membership through the 1920s. One noted family, spearheading the Spiritualist movement in 1848, was the infamous Fox Sisters. They emerged on the scene as three sisters who would communicate with the dead through a means of communicative knocks from the Other Side. The sisters held séances where they would call out letters of the alphabet and when a knock was heard, that was considered the intended letter. They continually repeated the process, moving on to the next letter of the message until the entire message was received.

As many more people became involved with spirit communication, the Spiritualists developed different methods and tools for doing so, but the most popular forums they used to demonstrate their mediumship abilities were through holding séances in homes, lecture halls and summer camp meetings. These believers were constantly looking for ways to expedite the communications with the spirits and found various ways to refine their communications, such as using

15

alphabet cards, direct channeling and automatic writing with a planchette or pencil.

In 1858, the planchette arrived in America after being discovered by an American spiritualist at séances he witnessed while visiting Paris. The word planchette is French, meaning "little plank." It is a flat piece of wood that sits horizontally, spreading its balance between two wheeled castors and a third "leg" that was an aperture for a pencil to be held. Automatic writing involved the operator placing one's hand on the planchette while the little wheels beneath allowed the little plank to move around freely, writing messages from the spirits. The planchette was a hit, rising in its popularity and prominence amongst the Spiritualists in America as it expedited the communication process with the spirits.

Automatic writing grew in its popularity post WWI due to the huge death toll. Countless loved-ones were lost to its carnage. The survivors wanted a way to reach out to the relatives they lost and connect with them through automatic writing's promise of communication with the spirits of the deceased.

Although automatic writing with the planchette was the craze for twenty-three years, it only took a back seat with the advent of the Ouija Board and its "new planchette" device. Yet, it was this French invention that was the predecessor to the reinvented planchette used with the Ouija Board. Talking Board and its pencil-less planchette became an even faster and more consistent tool for communicating with the spirits over the former days of scribbled, illegible writings the writing planchette would often produce.

Many automatic writers graduated from using the original, writing planchette device to holding a writing utensil within their fingers while trusting the free-flowing movements as the pen or pencil made its way across the page, providing messages from the Other Side. In our more recent history, the typewriter had been used to receive messages, as has the computer keyboard. In both instances, the typist allows the felt sensations in the fingers to guide them to which key to push next.

Pearl Curran popularized the Ouija Board's use as a divination tool in 1913. Through the Board she channeled a spirit known as Patience Worth, a 17th Century English woman. Curran, a middle class housewife who only completed the eight grade, produced prolific and remarkable bodies of writings, including poetry, plays and novels written in a Middle English dialect as she experienced Worth's communications. Originally, Worth communicated through the Ouija Board, but later Curran heard Worth's messages inside her head. She put aside the Board and turned toward dictating her messages for others to write as they came, as well as writing them herself with a pencil and later a typewriter. The spirit Patience Worth received accolades for her literature, including, being listed as one of the outstanding authors of 1918.

Throughout the years, there have been many others claiming that spirits communicating with them through the Ouija Board have been their source of writing and creative inspiration, and have guided them in their writing or channeled their entire body of work for them, as was the case with Pearl Curran. I too am such a person. I wrote my first published book, *The Spirit of Creativity: Embodying Your Soul's Passion* with the inspired and guided assistance of my spirit friends over the Ouija Board. They didn't dictate the book to me, instead we had sessions where we reviewed what I wrote and they made suggestions and gave input. Through these sessions, I was inspired to write specific sections and chapters in the book that were inspired by the topic of a communication we had just shared. At that time, I was told to write my first book from my soul to communicate its message. My Angel, Mary Angel said:

IT WILL BE YOUR KNOWING   OTHERS WILL HELP BRING IT OUT OF YOU   YOU MUST TAKE IT TO YOUR SOUL LEVEL BUT YOU MUST NOT WRITE ABOUT ME OR OUIJA

I mentioned in the introduction of this book, what you are reading is inspired by forty years of messages and experiences I have had with my spirit friends by means of my Ouija Board.

A couple of notable individuals who used the Board for their literary creations, includes poet James Merrill who channeled through Ouija all of his epic poems and won the Pulitzer Prize for Poetry in 1977, and the co-founder of Alcoholics Anonymous, Bill Wilson, who later claimed that the Ouija Board helped him create the infamous 12-step program.

Chapter 2 - Misconceptions: Jeer & Fear

KNOWLEDGE IS THE WAY SO WE CAN FIND TRUTH
- *The Higher Self*

The Bad Rap

With the invention of the Ouija Board, a new type of divination tool was conceived, entering the market and sweeping the nation. It was viewed and used throughout the early twentieth century as an entertaining, yet harmless parlor game. Originally, the Ouija Board was not associated with the occult, but when it did become associated, it fell from grace into a misleading path of misconception and landed into a fearful world of negative and demonic designations. Let's explore this further.

Although I believe this "bad rap" has been unfairly earned; nonetheless, it's a common public misconception to view Ouija with contemptuous ridicule and negative opinion. No sooner than the word "Ouija" is mentioned, most people respond with a quickly heightened jeer or fear. Very rarely do I encounter a neutral response. The response is almost always held in derision towards it, whether being one of mockery or one of fear. Let me tell you, I have heard the gamut of reasoning for why Ouija is bad, evil, scary or plain frivolous. Even given the negative response to its mere existence on a shelf or mention of it in a conversation, many people have had an experience with Ouija. Many have used one at some time within their life and typically, that was when they were young and at a sleepover or at a teen-age party with friends. In both examples, I would wager a bet that no one present during those susceptible years even had the slightest understanding of Ouija's complex dimension and intensity, let alone the extended complications that can arise from its improper use, when they were "messing around" with this "game." Shockingly enough, using a Ouija Board in this manner and within a disrespectful environment, anything and everything can and will go wrong, which I discuss later in this book. No wonder many people have the bejeebers scared out of them!

I find it amazing how many people have openly admitted to me to laying their hands on the Board, and of those who have, mostly they did so within a frivolous atmosphere, especially when they were young children at slumber parties. Others have admitted that they used the Board during their teen and college years, but during a party atmosphere and typically involving alcohol, but no matter when they used it, all have a story to share. A mail survey about the use of the Ouija Board that was published in *The Journal of Parapsychology* in September of 1999, explains that ninety percent of the participants

21

(mean age of 40) claimed "successful communications with a spirit," whereas sixty six percent claimed negative experiences. Out of all of the participants surveyed, a half of them felt compelled to use it. This speaks to their belief that "something" is happening and it's intriguing enough to try it. Parker Brother pushed a similar message by writing on their earlier-era Ouija boxes, "Weird and mysterious. Surpasses, in its unique results, mind reading, clairvoyance and second sight." Wooohooo...Whooohooo...Boo!

Using the Ouija Board as a "game" can attract either garbled and incoherent messages or mischievous entities that are typically earthbound and lost from the light. These entities can bring an entire host of poltergeist activity into the room (and into the lives) where Ouija is being played. Notice I use the word "play" when writing about the Ouija in this context. This is exactly what is happening. Ouija, the connective tool to the other side, is being "toyed with" in a mockingly fashion. This is a lot like the days when we were young and would pick up the telephone to crank-call people. That communication device, the telephone, was used for play and jokes. However, the person on the other end would either fall for the prank or hang up on us. The Ouija Board, not unlike a telephone, is also a communication device that links us to an unseen being(s) on the other end and brings forth a connection, thus communication. Yet, with this form of communication device, they don't necessarily hang up and we can't necessarily end the connection when we do not have an understanding of the energies we are evoking.

This is why Ouija is not a toy and is not for the spiritually weak and uninformed. When properly addressed, the Ouija is an opening to the greatest possibilities within the intended destinies of our souls. On the flip side, when used incorrectly, we evoke the dark side of the light, which truly encompasses all that we fear and can present itself as the negative influences many have reported experiencing as demonic and negative influences. Through our communications with our spirit friends, we learned that all we experience in life comes from our soul connection to All-That-Is, whether we chose to experience love or we chose to experience fear. The teachings continued to tell us that at every given moment, we choose to attract to us what we are within. Explained further by Ouija, via our ethereal* friend known as The Sun, we were told the meaning of its letters as an acronym during a session on April 27, 1996, he said:

OUIJA

O   ONENESS

U   UNIVERSE

I   INFORMATION

J   JOY

A   ALL

RELAX FIRST AND KEEP AN OPEN SOUL   AS NORMAL THIS OUIJA IS
NOT FOR THE WEAK   THIS IS IMPORTANT FOR ALL   THE SOUL IS
ALL THERE IS

Hasbro & Hollywood

It would be easy to just blame Hasbro and Hollywood for Ouija's
fall from the graces of a parlor room to a box in the back of a dark
closet somewhere, but I suggest that its public demise has been
contributed by a much larger influence.

Hasbro, the toy company who holds the rights to Ouija and owns
Parker Brothers as a subsidiary, states on their box, "It's only a game--
isn't it?" Brilliant marketing to children by suggesting that any
question they ask, Ouija will answer them. A tool that will provide
children the answers at a time when their parents still have ultimate
authority over their day-to-day destiny and control over the answers
the children are to have. Children and teenagers between the ages of
ten and twenty-five are still going through changes in their brains that
contribute to their important on-going development of their faculties.
The biggest change during this time is in the brain's part of the cortex
where cognitive and emotional information is processed. Their
developing thoughts, ideas and concepts during this formative time,

factor heavily into influencing the formation of their character and personality. I'm suggesting that at a time when one's identity is not fully formed, even unknowingly bringing about a negative experience from opening a portal is not a good idea without proper understanding of the consequences. Any warnings about this Board will only assist to keep a steady draw to it.

Hollywood loves to use the image of the Ouija Board or a likeness within their movies ever since its silver screen debut in 1973. Again, this was a brilliant marketing move, capitalizing upon all of the pop sensationalism and success Ouija had endured over the years from its popularity in use, demonstrated by its sales to the polarizing opinions people espoused. When Ouija was first produced by Parker Brothers in its first year, it outsold Monopoly, their most popular game of that day. William Fuld, the father of Ouija, was quoted saying that he had amassed profits totaling in three million during his years manufacturing and selling the Ouija Board. This was in 1920. Remember, he died in 1927 and this was before his family took over the business before selling to Parker Brothers in 1966. The first year of sales after Parker Brothers purchased the rights, they reported selling two million Boards in that one-year alone. Ouija obviously made its way into many homes.

With the release of the movie *The Exorcist* in 1973, Ouija became quickly notarized as a demonic tool. The scene in the movie shows Regan, who is the girl possessed by the demon Pazuzu, attempt communication via the Ouija Board with a Captain Howdy. The story indicates that Captain Howdy was the beginning of her possession before later being revealed as Pazuzu. Although the scene with Captain Howdy and the Ouija Board is about a minute long, it was long enough for pop culture to associate the Parker Brother's branded "mystifying game" as a feasible link to a darker influence and the possibility of possession. Capitalizing further upon this stigma, many Hollywood horror films continue to utilize Ouija's demonic stigma it received in 1973. Since then, Ouija and its distant relatives, other Talking Boards, have been used in countless movies, mostly horror films, but also including comedy, romance and drama movies.

Even given the negative and fearful connotations, the Ouija Board sustains itself as a pop icon, every-changing, along with our culture, and living on within our urban mythology. Even the name, Ouija, has become the catch-all-name to include all Talking Boards, much like Kleenex has become to denote all facial tissues. Even after all of these years, Ouija holds to its name, "The Mystifying Oracle" and keeps to its promise to provide, "...you entertainment you have never experienced...Unquestionably the most fascinating entertainment for modern people and modern life."

Fear

Fear is a big reason for Ouija being cast off into an oblivion of negativity. People often fear what they don't understand. It is easier to fear something than to take the time to learn about it. Fear is first and foremost created by assumptions. Assuming that all communications with the Beyond, coming from outside our typical experiences and the world of our everyday senses and faculties, is critically labeled ridiculous or blasphemous, is narrow-minded in itself. Just because these experiences can't be measured by scientific theory or understood by religious communities, speak to the unfair and harsh criticism Ouija Board has received. Quite often, this type of communication is attributed to ideomotor effects (involuntary and unconscious motor behavior) by the scientific community, while attributed to demonic and evil forces by many traditional Christians. Could there be a deeper reason for the ridicule and fear, thus the unfair judgment?

Platonic & Neo-Platonic Philosophy

To dig a little deeper into this fear, we need to review earlier schools of thought and divination practices that developed out of Platonic philosophy. Platonic doctrine, teaches us that the originality of anything and everything does not reside in the existence of the phenomenon or experience but exists within a universal and indestructible, essential form or idea. All essential forms and ideas come together and form the absolute, One Being, thus the supreme idea of the Good. In addition, Plato viewed philosophy as the ultimate practice to leave the body and reside in the soul. This higher state of conscious was achieved through mystical contemplation and self-discipline.

The early Greek and Roman Churchmen were greatly influenced by Plato's theory of ideas, particularly translating Plato's concept of the absolute, One Being, as being the One God. Other groups of thought were influenced by this doctrine as well, including the Neo-Platonists that contributed to the mystical aspects of Platonic thought. Neo-Platonists is a form of mysticism that teaches the origin of human soul as an emanation of its Supreme form, the One Being. It departs this existence to be in the world of phenomenon and experiences, but also teaches practical tools to work its way back to the Supreme Being. They believed that all things contain the divinity within themselves.

In 325 C.E., the Roman Emperor Constantine opened the Council of Nicaea and along with his bishops, made it clear that all Christians must believe their salvation could only be brought about through Christ's sacrifice for their sins, which would clearly distinguish Christians from the paganistic heresy of Platonic thought. This became the orthodox view for Christianity. They did not want to hear of talks about any higher truths of which to aspire. They expected that all salvation would come from the taking of the sacraments, the ceremonial drinking and eating of the flesh and blood of the Christ, by accepting one's salvation only through the Church.

Theurgy & Sciomancy

The early Christian tradition that inspired and developed from the Platonic and Neo-Platonic thoughts went underground to preserve what they believed were the original traditions of salvation, such as what they learned from great teachers like Jesus. This group is what we would come to know today as the Esoteric* Christians. Esoteric Christianity is to learn the mysteries of God. They believed through the practice of mystical teachings found in certain esoteric doctrines they could aspire to higher levels of consciousness. Under the teachings, one would work his way to being enlightened or initiated.

29

A tradition they would practice is one known as theurgy*, meaning "the science of divine works." In the teachings of theurgy, the mystic worked to invoke a higher source, as in one's Higher Self* and allow conversations and knowledge to be imparted with the goal of perfecting oneself. They believed that the tradition of theurgy would greatly benefit an individual as the practice united the individual with higher counterparts, taught spiritual wisdom and truths from a higher source, a divine consciousness, that couldn't be learned from man alone. Sciomancy*, a form of theurgy, was also practiced by various groups of early Esoteric Christians and Mystery traditions. In the practice of Sciomancy one communicates with the spirits of the dead or a spirit guide.

Nothing New Under the Sun

As the saying goes, "nothing new is under the sun" and that applies to the practical use of the Ouija Board. Talking Boards are modern inventions that have a deeply rooted past in humans' desire to connect with a source beyond for divination, insight, guidance and growth. Basically, all Ouija Board operators have been and are practicing a rudimentary form of theurgy or sciomancy. Could this be why there is research out there attempting to connect the Ouija Board back to Greece and China? Different mystery schools practiced theurgy, using many different techniques and tools over the ages. The ability to communicate with spirits or a higher part of one self for divination or spiritual advancement is what the Board also allows us to do, but to assume that the Board has a past in Ancient Greece or another ancient society has not been confirmed.

Spiritualism, from out of which sprang the Talking Board, is a very recent and modern day movement compared to the origination of Neo-Platonic, esoteric Christians. Yet the hands of time have passed the baton to the modern operators of the Talking Boards. We are using Ouija to either communicate with the spirits of the dead, as in sciomancy, or to communicate with our higher selves for spiritual gain, as in the practice of theurgy. Personally, I've been practicing both. In fact, for about four years, I only practiced the concept of theurgy by being in contact with the Board's Operators' and participants' higher selves for personal and spiritual growth. Over most of the other years, I was practicing the concept of sciomancy by communicating with strictly guides, ethereal beings and spirits of the deceased.

Get the Drift?

By connecting all of the historical dots presented, it's easier now to see how the Ouija Board has suffered its fall from grace into its bad rap. No different than the days of yesteryear when others were

31

persecuted if they didn't follow common thought decreed by the ruling faction. Etched into the psyche of traditional and orthodox Christians, is the doctrine set forth by the Council of Nicaea. In 325 BC, the practices and thoughts of those early Neo-Platonic Christians were abolished and demonized as being paganistic, thus considered a heretical practice that brought upon itself unduly, harsh punishment with unbearable consequences, including tortuous death. That is enough to frighten many people away from what they believe!

Adding fuel to the modern day fire, it doesn't help the cause that most of the leaders of today's science do not consider the hermetic practitioners of yesteryear who brought us their sciences, such as alchemy, sacred geometry and astrology as the true forefather's of the sciences we have today. The hermetic tradition developed in parallel to the Neo-Platonic philosophy and practice, and is also associated with the teachings and practices of a hidden wisdom, including the tradition of theurgy. Their science and practice is mostly considered blasphemous to the science world of today, not unlike the early Neo-Platonic Christians being considered heretics due to their theosophies and practices, beginning in the third century.

All of the traditions that went "underground" became associated with the occult, which translates to meaning, "knowledge of the hidden." To hide, Rightly so! Wouldn't you too wish to continue the practice that you found to be the truth within your life, the practice that opened you to a spiritual salvation attained from within yourself that brought you in touch with your soul? Occult took an a negative connotation to the ruling faction and during our modern era, the Ouija Board has been associated with occultism, with the "hidden." From this title, it carries a deeply rooted classification within humankind's psyche of mockery and chastisement.

Chapter 3 - My History with Ouija

IT'S ONLY A GAME—ISN'T IT?
- *Parker Brother's slogan*

The year was 1973, Bennie and the Jets was probably blaring over the radio, and I was playing Ouija Board with my girlfriends who lived down the street, the Johnson family sisters. Carey was my best friend and we would often hang out along with Brenda, her sister who was older by a year or so. Our fathers were in the military and we shared the Air Force life of always moving around, living everywhere and making new friends quickly. During this time, we were living on Kirtland Air Force Base in Albuquerque, New Mexico.

As mentioned in the Introduction of this book, I was already experiencing strange experiences for which I could barely communicate what these were and even when I tried, didn't really have a context in which to explain the oddities. After all, we lived on an Air Force base and there was always something flying above outside. So, when I saw colored lights outside my bedroom window at night that darted erratically one moment then hovered still without sound, my parents would explain this as just another military plane or helicopter.

I was becoming more and more inquisitive to trying to find a frame of reference for these light shows of the night, in addition to my many different room visitors, entering at night during the late sixties and into the middle seventies. My elementary library had a great section on the paranormal. Who knew that an elementary school would carry such books? I was thrilled and extremely interested. Being a voracious reader, I checked out every single one of those books, reading them while trying to understand my extraordinary encounters.

When Carey and Brenda pulled out a Ouija Board at their house one afternoon and suggested we try it, that made perfect sense to me, especially when they said you could talk to ghosts on it. Although I had not shared any of my visitations or encounters with my friends, I was interested in what this new tool could do. As I watched the planchette move underneath the weight of their fingertips, I thought to myself that they must have been pushing it. How could it be that easy to communicate with a ghost? They swore to me that it worked and invited me to try it with Carey shortly after they did their demonstration.

I remember the absolute silliness of the question when we did our first session together. Carey asked the Board, "How do you spell relief?" straight from that old television commercial about Rolaids. Under the gentle touch of our fingertips, which I was not pushing, the

35

Board spelled out: R O L A I D S. We laughed. But I still thought, this is a Board game, a Parker Brother's Board game, and to make it work, one of us must be pushing it. Now, I knew that I was not pushing it, so I could only assume that Carey must be pushing it. I made her swear that she wasn't. We continued our session, switching off between Carey being my partner and back to Brenda being my partner. I was entranced with its movement around the Board as it touched the letters and numbers, answering our questions. The answers came as one to three word answers and sometimes a small sentence. All the while, I was not pushing it and they swore they were not either, but I still wasn't sure what to think.

The Whammy!

Then the "whammy" came, the hook that led me on this forty-year Ouija Odyssey. I could feel the movement of the planchette change direction and speed and spell out the name of a girl I did not know, but said that she was the girls' sister who had died many years earlier and she was a twin to Brenda. I recall that she spoke to us just as if another girl friend of our age was sitting in the room with us. Now, I never even knew that Brenda was a twin nor did I know that her twin had died. What? My friends had a sister who was dead and we were speaking with her from the Beyond! This was crazy, yet very interesting nonetheless.

After my very first experience with this "game" and being able to speak with the Johnson girls' deceased sister, I was intrigued and excitedly ran home to tell my parents about what had just happened. Of course they didn't believe the story. They told me that someone was pushing it; the Board just does not work. Nevertheless, I convinced them to purchase one for me for Christmas that year and lo and behold, Santa Claus delivered! I was eight years old.

I continued to do Ouija sessions with Carey for a few more years while we still lived on base. Occasionally, I was branching out and experimenting with the Board with other friends too. We did this mostly during sleepovers and quite frankly, being silly with it. Although we did receive some direct messages, we also received silly information since we were operating on such a level. I also found that most of my younger friends over the years did not have the patience it required to develop a strong connection to spirits on the Other Side. Typically, my playmates would bore of it easily and grow tired and want to quit and play another game. I soon realized that not everyone else was as excited as I about the Board's implications for communication. Not everyone thought it was amazing that we were speaking to the deceased. Some of my friends were apparently told by their parents that it was an evil thing to be playing with and not to participate with me on the Board.

Eye-Opening

Now this was all very eye-opening to me, but I never assumed there could be a problem using it, as my parents allowed it. I never saw it as the antithesis to my religious upbringing. After all, we were practicing Catholics at the time, going to Church every Sunday, followed by Sunday school. In every bedroom we hung our cross. I went through my first holy communion and took the Eucharist during mass. We attended confession with the priests and had our own rosaries and could site the Acts of Attrition. How could this tool be evil, as I started hearing the references? All I was doing was learning about the other side and learning that the soul lives on. I was learning that we never lose our love ones. They all stay around and can still be with us, just that now, they were on the Other Side. To me this was groundbreaking information. I wondered why more people weren't tapping into this realm in this most simple of ways that I had discovered for myself via the Ouija Board.

Realizing that there was such a negative connotation associated with the Board, I went underground with it, meaning, I rarely shared or spoke about it with anyone, let alone all of my friends. Instead, just shared my little Ouija secret with a few select people over the years whom I could trust, and would share these experiences and invite them to try this form of communication with me. This continued until I was a senior in college.

As I continued my work with the Board on and off throughout childhood and through my teenage years and into my college years, the Board was used more or less as a novelty. It was fun, playful and slightly scary. Scary in the sense that we didn't understand the mystery of it all and we purposely called on dead people we knew and allowed those we didn't know to also come through. Pretty much, I had developed an opening, a portal, through which many varying entities could enter and communicate. Although, doing this, I was never afraid of it. I always knew that when I wanted to and felt the need to, I could just put the Board away and tuck it back into my closet with my other games.

Out of the Closet

It wasn't until Christmas break from college in 1986, while staying at home with my family that one of my brothers asked me to get that old Ouija Board of mine out of the closet, as he wanted to try it again. We had not engaged with it together in several years. He said he wanted to use it because earlier in school that week, one of his high school teachers let them mess around with the Board during class. I was slightly surprised to hear that he was using it in High School as a senior and their teacher permitted this. I asked him if it worked for them. He told me that it was working for them and wanted to pursue it more with me.

I pulled the Board out and we sat down on the floor in the privacy of my bedroom with legs crossed, the Board spanning our laps. We simply asked to speak to whom was there. That is when we met Ectua and Wilma Jean.

Ectua identified himself as knowledgeable in psychology and came across as being very pompous. I, who was studying psychology and planned to go to graduate school to become a psychotherapist, was taken aback by his denigrating comments. As he communicated with us, he spoke at us and belittled my current level of understanding of psychology. I directly told him that he could not speak to me that way and that he must be respectful to speak with us or I would put the Board away and he would be done communicating. Apparently, he didn't like the control seat I was sitting in and began cursing at us on the Board. He expressed many expletives as the planchette erratically moved around the Board with such force, causing it to fly off the Board several times.

My brother and I quickly grew quite bored of Ectua and his nonsensical cussing and told him we were done. I picked up the Board, told him he could never come back to speak with us again, wiped the Board off and we started the session again with our fingers resting on the planchette at the middle of the Board. In steps Wilma Jean.

Wilma came through in a very strong manner, meaning, she could clearly move that planchette around the Board and the way it moved, it had a solid feeling about it. She didn't care for Ectua either and waited in the wings to enter. Wilma was entertaining and informative. She explained to my brother and me that she was last living as a slave. She was a cotton picker in the Deep South. She was warm to us always on the Board as she shared accounts from her life. Wilma liked speaking with us and we liked speaking to her. She became the first spirit we allowed to enter the Board on every occasion we used the Board.

She became friendly with my brother and me during our sessions, engaging with us as if she was right there in person. She'd ask about our day and share more about her life. No matter what was going on or how hard of a life she experienced, she was always positive and uplifting. Little did I know that she would become one of my first teachers on the Board about the seriousness nature and purpose for this tool, I once was told was only a game.

41

Ouija Goes to College

I returned to college for my last semester of my senior year with my Ouija Board in tote. I could hardly wait to show my sorority sisters the fun and interesting message I had been receiving, let alone that I was communicating with a ghost. As crazy as that might have sounded to some, I didn't care, I was gleaning all kinds of fascinating information from Wilma Jean about the other side and life between lives. She shared her understanding of reincarnation, explaining that all of us continue to come back to new lives with the same souls we knew before. Whenever we opened the Board, Wilma served as its "mistress of ceremony" as we spoke to other spirits and asked specific questions. She was my first "gatekeeper" to the other side and I could tell that our connection and communication was growing stronger. She was the first to enter the portal, help messages come through from other spirits, guide others into the portal to communicate and she was the last to leave and help us close the opening.

Once I returned to college, I started doing the Board with a sorority sister and close friend named Linda who could fully "let go" and "allow" the process of this type of often, laborious form of communication. Linda had a Board that was older than mine and a lot larger. We really liked using her larger Board that had belonged to her older siblings and been in their family since the fifties or sixties. Wilma Jean liked this larger Board too. She told us so.

Linda could sit with me for several hours at a time while we did our sessions. Wilma was still our Other Side leader. Word began to spread around the University Campus, specifically Greek Row, that Karen and Linda were the witches of the sorority house, communicating with the dead. Next thing I heard was that another fraternity was claiming that they were in communication with Wilma Jean too via their Ouija Boards. Wilma Jean told me that it simply was just not true, as she only spoke to my partners and me on the Board. She was adamant about this, as she and I had supposedly shared a past incarnation together. After all, it was our friendship after all of these years and lives that kept our bond.

These were strange, yet amazing times, in that we inadvertently started a subculture movement down Greek Row of working with the Board and speaking to spirits. These were also unfathomable times because we were experiencing hard core communications with ghosts, while learning the interconnectedness between the living and the dead. I learned about the ever so slight shift of energy that allowed communication to unfold and what created earth bound spirits and poltergeist activity. I learned that we existed in an energy field that was boundless, timeless and nonlocal and by just tuning our intentions, not unlike tuning a radio dial to bring in another frequency, we changed our frequency and matched a similar frequency. I was beginning to feel like maybe my major was not in psychology after all, but instead in physics and the study of frequency and time travel.

Wilma Jean stayed with me through all of these teachings and would willingly take a side seat when other new spirits started coming through. She often told me that this was just part of the learning I was to undertake as I progressed on my spiritual understanding of the Other Side.

January of 1987, Anne King enters the portal. She was out there waiting to be recognized, so she tells me. She didn't want to die. I heard the story about her being in our sorority and dying in a car wreck way too soon and way before her personality was ready to leave her physical incarnation. I purposely called upon her via the Ouija Board. I felt that we had a bond of fraternal sisterhood, as she had lived in the sorority house several years before I lived there. She was very accomplished at a young age and I heard how her life was just stripped from her in that car wreck. I figured it's better to speak with a human who had recently passed over, than a person who had passed many, many years ago. Boy was I wrong!

Anne came through immediately. She was funny and friendly and loved to talk and be heard. Again, just like other entities with whom I

44

communicated before her, she was as easy to speak with as if she was a friend sitting in the same room with us. She recounted fun stories about college life, the fraternity parties and sorority sisterhood. When she began to tell me stories about some of her best friends who I knew were active sorority Alumnae, I truly paid attention. Now, there was finally proof to my communications with the dead. She could recount in great detail the fun stories with names, dates and the events. At this time I thought, "Now I can do some serious corroboration of the stories Anne is telling us."

During one such session in which I purposely inquired about fun stories she could tell us about her life when she lived at the sorority house, she told Linda and me all about her fun with Marie, who was an active alumna within our chapter. When Marie was in college, she also lived in our sorority house and was a dear friend, if not one of Anne King's best friends in the sorority. Anne told us that she would like to speak with Marie again and requested that we invite her to our room for one of our sessions. At this time, we were operating the Ouija Board at least three to four times per week. These were very interesting times to say the least.

So, after a chapter meeting one Monday night, we invited Marie into our room and shut the door. Linda and I told her that what we were about to tell her would blow her mind and that with the utmost of respect for her, did not share any of this information with others at this time, which we were about to share with her. I spoke in whispers as I said to Marie that we had been communicating with the ghost of Anne King and that Anne has been telling us fun stories about the adventures she and Anne once shared. The look on Marie's face said it all. In disbelief she said, "sure, right."

Then I began telling her the details from earlier sessions with Anne King. She wanted to know how I knew such things. She had kept much of these adventures private and only shared them with Anne because they experienced them together. I mean, Anne was sharing the "dirt" on their adventures together. I further told her that Anne requested that they have a conversation. Marie was dumbfounded now, but we had her undivided attention. Linda and I pulled out the large Ouija Board and welcomed Anne to the Board. The planchette launched around the Board in excitement, spelling so very quickly, I could hardly keep up with the words. She recounted story after story to Marie with great details. Marie looked up at us and told us to "quit this joke." I explained this is not a joke; this is real communication with her deceased friend, Anne. There was no way I could have known their private, intimate details of what types of shenanigans they were pulling over at the Sigma Chi house a decade earlier! Marie was laughing and crying while the Board told the tales of their adventures.

Anne would even laugh on the Board too as she spelled out the laughter. Marie only did that one session with us, although Anne asked us to give Marie little messages every now and then when we saw her.

I wasn't always sure what the best way was to approach people about messages I received to give them or the information I was learning. So when Marie never returned to speak further with Anne, I felt it best to just drop my burning question, "why would Marie not want to speak to her friend anymore?" Again, I was reminded that crossing through this barrier between the living and the dead and receiving messages was not a common dinner table topic or an experience to be accepted by the mainstream populace, let alone friends and colleagues!

Where does this type of "shut down" response leave me along with all of this amazing information I was learning about the other side? What does this mean for the future of Ouija and ghost whispering? Why aren't people as excited about this form of communication as I am? Don't people want to know that life continues to exist and we never really die? I had an entire host of questions that was driving me crazy, yet nonetheless, I continued in my pursuit, finding other interested people to be Ouija Operators with me, so I could continue these enlightening sessions and continue my education into the paranormal. It was from these Ouija experiences and not from my

47

college training that I learned of my insight into the world as being so much richer than we can perceive with the naked eye and so much larger than we can even try to comprehend with our minds. Life and death were inseparable, instead they were both just different sides to the same fascinating coin and I had found this rare coin. I was happy to be carrying it in my pocket. Now, my life was enriched in meaningful ways.

Chapter 4 - The Proper Use

TRUST IN LOVE AND EACH OTHER
- *The Higher Self*

My Turning Point

It was during my college days, I was twenty-one years old and thirteen years beyond my first experience using the Ouija Board with the Johnson sisters, when I stumbled upon the healing powers of a Ouija session. Now, I had experienced some mind-blowing, goose-bumping, spine-chilling and spectacular sessions, but I had never experienced a session as I am going to recount for you right now. This session was my turning point, that moment in time when I knew without a doubt, the importance of doing the Ouija Board and the direction I must take it.

It all started when I invited a group of my sorority sisters into our downstairs chapter room to witness a session with Ouija. Several of these girls were feeling anxious and scared about my use of the Ouija. A few were also Catholics and told me that I was partaking in something bad and evil and that there is no way this tool could even work. It was inferred that I must be pushing it, along with my Ouija Partner, and making up the stories they were hearing. They really wanted to give me the benefit of the doubt, so when I invited them to come downstairs into our special sorority meeting room, they agreed to come and watch, but swore they would not touch it.

"Not a problem," I told them, as only Linda and I would be touching the planchette while Dena would serve as the scribe, writing as the words would be spelled out across the Board. Not only was I going to show them that the Ouija worked, but I went one step further and told them that Linda and I would operate the Board blind-folded since we both had that much confidence in the Board and it's ability to communicate with us. Plus, I wanted to prove to them that we only served as the channel, so to speak, that the entities would use, communicating through their movements of the planchette as it moved around the Board. We couldn't see or know what it would be writing. By the way, this was the first and only time to this date that I felt the need to operate the Ouija Board blind-folded, as I felt the need to prove what we were doing back then. Since that moment in time, I have not felt the need to ever prove anything like this again. I'm telling you, this session forever changed me!

So, after all the girls had congregated to our session, with doors closed and with at least 8-10 girls gathered around Linda and me, we sat on the floor, crossed-legged with the Board perched across our laps, we tied on our blindfolds. I made sure I couldn't see out at all and

I asked Linda to do the same. Dena was sitting adjacent to us on the floor with a pad of paper and pen, ready to write whatever Ouija was to spell.

I opened the session by asking Wilma Jean if there was a message for anyone in the room and if so, to allow it to come through. What happened next, was the kind of thing that happens when you feel a truth so profoundly, but so out of your normal experience, that you choose not speak of it again, only because it's shocking and to grasp it would mean that one's worldly perceptions might have to change. (Bingo! This is probably what happened to Marie as well.)

With blindfolds on, the planchette began to move around the Board in a most energetic and rapid manner. Truly, it was all I could do to maintain contact with my fingertips on the planchette. I felt sorry for Dena because I knew that she had to be writing so very quickly that she couldn't look down at the paper, but only keep her eyes focused on the next letter the planchette would point to. Voraciously, crazily, quickly, but with accuracy, the planchette whirled around that Board with determination. I knew it was a different entity than the ones to whom I was generally speaking. It's as if each entity has its own way of moving and a current, if you will, like a unique pattern, that is specific for each visitor on the Board. After doing the Board for a while, you pick up on the subtle nuances such as this.

51

While the Board was spelling frantically, I heard a slight whimper and gasp. I asked if all was okay without removing my blindfold and without understanding anything that was being communicated across the Board. I received a confirmation back from one of the girls to continue. The planchette continued its frenzied movements all over the Board and then came to an abrupt stop. I knew the communication was over, so I asked Linda to remove her blindfold while I did too.

We then turned to Dena and asked her to read the message, which at this point, Dena said she did not know what it wrote as it was moving so quickly and all she could do was write fast without looking down.

This is the gist of what Dena read out loud to us:

HELLO LINDSEY   THIS IS YOUR SISTER   I AM FINE   TELL MOM AND DAD THAT I AM FINE   SO IS MY BOYFRIEND   WE LOVE YOU ALL WE ARE STILL WITH YOU   WE FELT NO PAIN AND DIED ON IMPACT THE ONLY PAIN WE EVER FELT WAS THE PAIN THE FAMILY FELT AND EXPRESSED AT OUR FUNERALS   WE ARE AT PEACE AND FEEL LOVE   PLEASE DO NOT BE CONCERNED ABOUT US ANYMORE KNOW THAT WE LOVE YOU AND WILL ALWAYS BE WITH YOU   WE WILL BE WITH YOU AGAIN   I LOVE YOU ALL

There was not a dry eye in the room. The Catholic girls were shocked, amazed and didn't know what to say. For that matter, no one really knew what to say. I broke the ice and said, "Lindsey, I didn't know that you had a sister who died in a car accident." At this point, Lindsey was bawling, you know, one of those intensely deep cries that rattles your gut and chokes your breath. She couldn't speak. She just nodded her head. While Lindsey cried deeply, all of us sat there with her, allowing these intense emotions to be expressed without trying to make it better or silence her or say much more of anything. I thought to myself, "How could one message have such an impact on all of us?"

Internally, I realized the therapeutic impact that such a session could have on a person receiving the message, allowing them to feel, to express pent up emotions from a painful event and to receive the gift of closure. I was amazed at the impact such a session could have on an entire group of people too. That's when I realized, the messages aren't just for the intended subject; they hold a much greater purpose than that. They are for all who are present since all of us will face dying, death, terrible accidents, hardship and eternal love.

When Lindsey was finally able to speak, she said that she and the rest of her family had always hoped that her sister did not feel the pain when she died from that horrific car accident. She said that she would share the message with her parents and her other sister. The relief and "free-ing" of her spirit I witnessed that moment was intense, an eye-opener and a heart gripper. I told the group that now Ouija could be

53

used as a tool to heal. In that moment, I was forever changed and everyone left that room a different person, all the while, doing what they must with what they just witnessed, received and learned.

I realized that Ouija is not for those who are content living within the confines of narrow-mindedness. It can create fear when misinterpreted; yet heal hearts when allowed to do its job. This session was the golden egg and I was determined to share the richness this tool can bring when used within the right context.

Uh Oh; Now What?

Now, I had a purpose for Ouija. No longer was it a novel experience, talking to any spirit passing by the portal; no, that was not for me any longer. Now, I knew that I was to educate others about Ouija, help others find closure with loved ones who has passed and receive guidance from their ancestors and spirit guides. Also, I knew we could use it to learn about past lives and what happens when someone dies and what happens when they are dead and in between lives. We could expand our minds, enrich our lives and tap into the human existence here and beyond.

I decided that if I am only going to engage with the Ouija Board in a serious nature, then I would create a sacred space that helps shape the seriousness of the session and helps set the intention of our upcoming session before we started each session. I had read enough spiritual books about the positive benefits of prayer, meditation and intending positive thoughts that I knew if I employed a similar practice to create an atmosphere of seriousness and reverence around the use of the Board, I should be able to be met with the same type of focus from my spirit friends on the other side.

To take this one step further, I thought to myself, I will treat this work as sacred. After all, I saw what profound affect the message had on Lindsey and also on her deceased sister who so wanted to communicate with her family and relieve the pain they still felt in their hearts. Lindsey needed this message and relief as much as her deceased sister needed to impart this message. I began to understand that healing and growth never end. Even in our death, we are still loving, evolving and healing ourselves and so are the ones with whom we are connected, whether they are incarnate or discarnate. Nothing truly separates us other than our own beliefs, stemming from what we have learned up to that point. If I could use Ouija sessions to help others experience this, then the only reasonable way I must work the Board now, was under this guiding notion.

Once I fully understood the profound healing nature of my work with the Ouija Board communications, I knew that I must always approach this work from a space of reverence. Not unlike my work as a psychotherapist, it was my role to create a safe and supportive space for my clients, a space that promoted an opening up and deepening of their emotions, thoughts and insights. This space was made safe by having a consistent beginning and ending, typically an hour to an hour and a half time limit. The therapy space was further made safe through my nonjudgmental presence as a client opened up. By being fully present and aware, I could listen and truly hear; I could be empathic and authentic. All of this is like a domino effect, creating a space in which the client could allow herself to deepen into her own truths and awareness. It was as if I became more of a witness and a guide, promoting and allowing truths to be exposed, but only be abruptly direct when I heard or saw "past behaviors" come to the surface that were troublesome and maintaining her from affecting healthy change within her evolving life. So, I figured that I must treat the Ouija Session in the similar manner if I wanted to endeavor profound change.

Session Preparation

When preparing for your Ouija session, it's important to understand what you will attract to your session spirits that are resonating at a similar level and at the same vibration quality of your thoughts, feelings and behaviors that you hold. I will further explain how to prepare and establish positive Ouija communications by explaining why and then how to prepare your internal, external and spiritual spaces. Also, I will advise to other factors that will be out of your control, but nonetheless, their influence must be understood.

The Internal Space

We need to prepare not only the physical space for a Ouija session, but most importantly, prepare our own internal space, our vibration, for a Ouija session. The internal space includes, our mindset, our emotions and our spiritual and physical needs. We need to make sure we are vibrating in alignment with our intentions for the session. Not only is it paramount to have positive intentions set for the communication, I can't stress enough how you must be prepared for this interaction emotionally, environmentally and spiritually.

Throughout the years, I have developed a system to help my mind, my feelings, my body and my transcendent self relax into a clear and open space that promotes positive experiences with the Ouija Board communications. From Quantum's Law of Energy, I understand everything that is beyond the basic elements vibrates to its own unique, vibrational blueprint. This vibrational blueprint is comprised from a unique combination of the vibratory variables that exist in wave energy, such as the frequency, the pattern, the speed and the regularity of the wave. This frequency is known as electromagnetic

57

wave (ELM) energy. With every pulse of our ELM energy, we broadcast and we attract. This is our energy field, a field we are solely responsible for that transmits our vibrations, while magnetizing other similar vibrations into our energy field.

All of us know what it's like to be in a room with an angry or negative person, whether it stems from yourself or from another. The tension in the room feels intense and thick, like you could cut it with a knife. The ambience remains and starts to spiral down as others get caught up in the negativity, the anger, and then the complaining starts. If you must stay in the room, such as a business meeting, then the only way to cut the tension is to literally cut yourself away from the negativity and internally shift yourself into a positive attitude and outlook. The Institute for HeartMath* explains how to do this by stopping yourself, relaxing for a few minutes, then imagine breathing a neutral attitude into your heart or chest area. As you breathe, you quiet the negative feelings and re-center yourself in your heart. You shift your experience and bring it back into what HeartMath calls a "heart-coherent" state. Their research measure the heart's electromagnetic (ELM) energy field and studies the effects of heart coherence on the individual and within their social environment. They discovered that the electromagnetic signal generated by the heart could influence the brainwaves of another person when they interact, suggesting that this exchange between heart-brain is influenced by our emotions. Emotions are the key to influencing our environment.

This is very similar to what happens when we work with energy, such as communicating with entities and consciousness that are around and beyond us, but nonphysical. If you approach the session with a negative, facetious or frivolous attitude, you jade and influence the communication and experience to the same quality that matches the level of those intentions. After all, you the physical being, have opened the communication within a specific ELM energy and you will be met with a similar frequency. I recommend that you fine-tune your ELM energy by establishing and anchoring positive intentions into your heart center and take responsibility for the emotional space you are creating for your Ouija session.

The External Space

Setting up the external space for a Ouija session is really no different than setting up for a counseling session. You must have a beginning and an ending protocol for the session. You must remain open to allow communication to come through and be willing to receive messages that may take some time to develop. You must be patient as the messages come through and be clear about the type of communication that will be allowed within the session. Basically, setting boundaries to a session is important for anything of substance to come through.

I will first list all of the components to a session and then address how to attend to each one.

1.) Set a date/time for a session

2.) Come to the set session after you release any distractions

3.) Light a candle or burn incense that reminds you of each session being sacred

4.) Sit in a comfortable position

5.) Take a few moments and make deep & clearing breaths, while releasing any present tensions and distractions

6.) Now breathe with intentions to relax and center yourself within your hips (*See Section: Hips to Heart Breathing on page 69.*)

7.) Next, breathe into and through your heart until you can feel the heart open

8.) The main spokesperson (who will also be the speller) for the session takes the hands of the Ouija partner and holds their hands while stating a prayer, incantation or intention for the session. (*See Section: Suggested Opening Protective Prayer on page 71.*)

9.) Now, you are ready to start the session. Place your fingertips on the planchette and allow its movement, trusting its movements while you relax.

10.) Once moving, for ease of communication, request that it lands on the letter, number or word (yes/no) until the speller[1] states the letter, number or word out loud.

11.) Once you or the spirits are finished with the communication, always end the session with gratitude and thanks for the communication from the other side and the entities with whom you spoke.

12.) Then, with fingers still on the planchette, say goodbye to close the portal of the Board.

13.) Put the Board away and close the circle of all that are present by blowing out the candle or stubbing the burning incense. This way, the space is closed; you remove yourself from the sacred and return to the secular, metaphorically and literally.

---

[1] I suggest that only one person serve as the main speaker and that same person serve as the speller, stating the letters, numbers, words out loud. This way you develop a consistent protocol for managing a session's communication.

The Ambiance - Bringing it All Together

I will further explain the "lucky number" thirteen steps listed previously and incorporate them into the Internal Space suggestions. It is imperative that you fully grasp the importance of creating an energetic field around these sessions. This will make all of the difference between creating a session of negative or fear-producing results or creating a positive session by taking spiritual responsibility to receive enlightened responses. Not only is it paramount to have positive intentions set for the communication, I can't stress enough how you must be prepared for this interaction physically, emotionally, spiritually and environmentally.

Schedule the Session

When you establish a set date and time for your Ouija Session, this immediately establishes a serious nature about your upcoming session for you, your Ouija Board partners and any others who will be attending the session. You can still do an impromptu session, but I suggest from many years of experience, the scheduled sessions bring about much better results and often, much more communication, especially when you are new to this tool. I believe it works better because as you wait for the intended day and time to approach, you are anticipating the session and allowing quandaries to spin around in your thoughts. Once you have established contact with your main spirit guides, they are paying attention to your thoughts proceeding a scheduled session because they know you want to make contact and will be eager to allow communication.

Elevate Your Senses

In order to begin a session, you must create a sacred space. A sacred space is a place you ceremonially enter and once there, you are only there for the intended purpose and when you exit, you ceremoniously close the space, all the while keeping it revered. This is no different that what any healer would do when providing their services. A shaman, priest, yogi, medicine woman, psychic, therapist or hypnotherapist, to name a few, would have a space they have created that you enter. Depending upon their belief system and practice, they could possibly douse the space with sage, burn incense, state a prayer, have you state repetitious words or close your eyes and leave the secular and enter the sacred. The idea is that a sacred space has been created through incorporating the senses, by removing the thoughts and feelings of the day and replacing them with new senses that take you into a new space. This sacred space could be the psychoanalyst's couch where you free-associate your feelings, to entering the church where service is about to begin and making the sign of the cross with the holy water as you enter, to closing your eyes as the hypnotherapist helps you relax by way of your breath into the deeper brain frequencies. Ultimately, each practitioner helps you transport from one space into another.

You set the space with the Ouija session in a similar fashion. Setting the stage of respect and reverence, while creating a consistent ritual such as, lighting a candle, saying a prayer and breathing deeply to relax and open to receptivity is how you can use your senses to move into a receptive place for communication.

Breathe to Ground & Open Yourself

Just as you would use rhythmic breathing in a yoga session to relax and deepen yourself into the poses, you use your breath to relax and deepen your receptive centers to open and allow this unique form of communication. As you breathe full belly breaths, imagine the type of breath that emanates from your diaphragm and pushes your belly out and then allows your shoulders to drop and your belly to deflate on the release of the breath. While doing this, you will be able to feel yourself release your daily routine and relax into the present moment, into the session at hand. The better you can stay focused in the present moment with a Ouija session, the better the communication will be.

Such deep and methodical breaths not only help you relax and prepare for your session, they serve as power stress reducers. When you can slow yourself down through the deep breathing, you calm you senses, you heighten your awareness, you release toxins and you slow down your autonomic nervous system, which provides a myriad of health benefits to boot.

Respect for Yourself & the Spirits

When you work with the Ouija Board, you have a responsibility to approach it with a caring, respectful attitude. The responsibility is yours when you start opening the channels between you and the unseen forces and energies. I warn you to only go into this space if you vow to treat yourself, the spirits and the session with the same type of respect any other healer or practitioners of the spiritual arts would do, in a reverent manner. Once you open to this type of experience, you are responsible to protect and not cause harm to yourself and any others within the proximity of your session and the work. Working with the Ouija with such respect, will only garner a caliber of respect from the entities and consciousness with whom you will be in communication. Respect breeds respect. After all, doesn't everyone and everything with a conscious awareness respond much better and thrive within mutual care and respect? Humans do, animals do and the plant kingdom does too!

Opening the Portal

Opening and closing the portal of our consciousness is paramount for a healer to be able to affect change. Ouija communication works in the same manner. We must set the space, open the space in which we will inhabit during the session and close the space with the same type of reverent manner. Not only will we open the space for ourselves, but we will also open the portal for communication with the Beyond in a similar fashion.

Opening and closing the portal of communication with the Board is no different than how a shaman, healer, psychic, therapist or hypnotherapist would start and end their sessions. The idea is that when you enter another realm, you must ask permission, be respectful, practice patience and then leave it in the same way you found it, with respect, honor and appreciation. Once you are relaxed from your deep breathing, state out loud the Opening Protective Prayer I have included in this chapter for your use.

Closing the Portal

Think of closing the portal as a process of actually returning full circle to what you said, felt and requested when you opened the portal.

So, you mentally return to your stated intentions and purpose of the session and state out loud your thanks to the spirits and those in the session for their focus and communication about your topics of interest. You thank them for any other knowledge and wisdom gleaned. You reiterate that the white light closes the portal and surrounds you, the other session attendees and the spirits as you say goodbye. While stating all of this out loud, your fingers are still on the planchette. Don't be surprised if there is still movement around the Board or a few mores words are spoken. The spirits may just stop or they sometimes leave the session by moving the planchette down to the Goodbye on the Board. Once you close it, you are done and now, you can return to your secular life.

Patience with the Process

When you first begin to work with the Board, you will find that it will take many hours of session time under the fingers to finally find all of the elements coming together to create a decent session with precise communication. The process requires coming to the Board for each session, following the guidelines stated above and remaining calm and patient while you work the Board with your partner. Now, each partner you do the Board with will produce different learning curves, thus different results. As with anything you do in life, the axiom "practice makes perfect," also pertains here.

At first the communication will struggle with its spelling and will provide jumbled messages that will require you asking the Board for further clarification, but with consistency, practice and patience, you will be able to deepen the communication into clear and concise words and sentences. You will also notice the speed increasing in which the planchette moves about the Board and spells.

One habit to avoid that I have witnessed many novices do while using the Board, is to ask just yes and no questions. The longer you continue to ask yes and no questions, the longer it will take for the entities on the other side to develop the ability to communicate through the portal, the planchette and ultimately your energy, as you touch the planchette to learn to spell. So, as a good teacher would do with her student, she would allow the time needed for the entity to learn to use the planchette to spell. Again, practice patience!

I will only use the yes and no type of responses when I have already asked a question and need a slight clarification at the level of checking on the spelling or meaning of a word or to ask if that is what they meant. I do all I can to refrain from yes and no questions, as my goal is to develop the ability for the spirit to learn to spell and to garner paragraph type answers.

Hips to Heart Breathing

There is a special type of breathing exercise I developed from my work with Ouija and then practiced it within my personal meditations and journaling sessions. Once I began experiencing the results of this type of connective breathing, I taught it to the other Ouija Board Operators and all others attending the sessions. This technique quickly grounds and relaxes the breather by promoting an opening of the heart chakra for authentic and receptive communication.

I suggest that you try implementing this meditative breathing into your session as well. It has so profoundly influenced me that it is the cornerstone of my next book's philosophy that I am currently writing. Use this technique when you deeply breathe, preparing for a Ouija session. Have the other participants and Board Operator do the same. Take your time until all are in that same coherent heart space that HeartMath teaches. Then you are ready to state the Opening Protective Prayer. Be ready for incredible messages to follow.

Here is the breathing technique explained in the form of a guided meditation:

As you sit in your space, preparing for your session, bring your attention to your breath. Take your breath into a longer and a slower breathing pattern and as you do so, imagine yourself dropping your focus, your awareness, into the fullness of your sacrum, your pelvis, your hips. Breathe into this space with your long, methodical breaths to drop all of your weight into this location, allowing your shoulders and rib cage to drop as well. Breathe and center into the seat of your hips, your throne. Once you feel relaxed within this space, bring the awareness of your breath into your chest, into your heart area. All the while, your hips remain centered and grounded in your throne. Now, breathe out of your heart as if your heart can breathe. As it breathes, it opens, and as it opens, it relaxes. Continue breathing into this space and relaxing into the expansion within yourself within your heart space. Now, imagine the feeling of love breathing into this space with each in-breath and then imagine the same feeling emanating out with each out-breath. Relax. Breathe. Feel. Allow.

You only need to take a couple of minutes with this breathing exercise. Over time and with repetitious practice, you may start to feel a warm vibration arise from within your body, intensifying within this space of your heart. This is all good. This is your intuitive heart, opening and expanding within your conscious awareness. It is this experience you will bring into the session and it is this awareness I encourage you to further develop. I will speak more about developing this awareness in the section on *Your Spiritual Practice, page 78*. Once centered within your heart space, you are ready to state out loud the Opening Protective Prayer as provided next.

Opening Protective Prayer

This Opening Protective Prayer is a rendition of the prayer I use within all of my sessions and I encourage you to start with this one. Once you have established communication and are comfortable with this process of opening the session, then craft your opening prayer, incantation, meditation to work within the parameters of your own language and style. Components to include in the Opening Protective Prayer are:

- Visually imagine and verbally state that a protective light surrounds each other, the space, the Board and all that comes through this Board in communication.

- Next state that only that which comes from this place of illumination, truth, clarity and wisdom can come through this portal of communication.

- State that only that which is of the white light is welcome.

This is a version of mine that I present to you to use, which came from the original prayer I developed on January 23, 1995 for my protective use with the Board:

Dear God, Goddess, Universe, Spirit* and all of our relations and guides. We welcome you to our circle today. As we do so, the white light surrounds each one of us present within this sacred circle where we come together, including the Board, the portal and all that comes through this connection. White light surrounds us and protects us, including the house, (stating the names of any other people or animals within the home), ourselves, our vehicles as we return to our own homes and back into our own individual lives. We only ask that those from within the while light, those of universal knowledge and wisdom, and those who seek universal truth, to come forward in our communications. We have items of topic for which we would like to discuss and welcome the messages that ensue. We honor and thank you in advance for these teachings. The white light is with us. We may now begin.

Atmospheric & Planetary Effects on a Session

There are many conditions within our control and influence when we set up and manage a session, however there are other environmental conditions we cannot influence, such as atmospheric and planetary events. Also take into consideration there are these influencing factors when trying to initiate a session, as these types of factors will affect the level and capability for the spirits to communicate. It seems strange to think that the weather or certain planetary alignments can affect a Ouija Board session, but I have discovered that they can and do.

To understand this better, I use the example of a wireless device, such as the current cell phones we use today. In simplistic terms, a cell phone is basically a two-way radio that transmits a radio signal to the wireless company's tower that recognizes the identity of the phone through the signal and in turn provides a radio frequency that allows your calls to be sent and received. A cell phone may not work at certain times given specific conditions, such as the signal being out of range of a tower or the signal being obstructed by tall buildings and other structures, natural and manmade, like hills and vegetation. Communication can also drop or not connect at all due to high call volume on the nearest tower. Atmospheric conditions can negatively affect a cell phone's radio signal, such as thunderstorms, wind, moisture or lack of moisture in the air and solar flares.

Using the Ouija Board is like placing or receiving a cosmic wireless phone call. We are calling out and "they" are calling back from another space, another dimension and another frequency. I have discovered some of the same atmospheric reasons that affect cell phone transmission, effecting Ouija's communication in a similar fashion. The spirits have even come on the Board announcing the inability to do our scheduled session due to the energy at hand, meaning they are having problems with communicating due to planetary alignment and its magnetic affects.

These are the conditions of a session we cannot control. Even though you may do everything accordingly as I suggest and recommended previously, a session may still not work. It may be that you won't receive any movement or the movement could be very slow and heavy. At other times, you may just receive gibberish. You may receive a quick message and reason, if fortunate, why there is not any communication today. There is really nothing you can do about this, but wait this out, unless you can control the weather or alignment of planets! The Ouija spirits have told me before that when the atmospheric energy is "not right" they can't communicate. The following examples provide more detail about how this information is communicated to us.

7/18/94 – At the beginning of a session a warning came through, it said, "JUPITER BECAREFUL TONIGHT   YOU WILL SOON SEE." Not understanding what this meant, the Big One entered the Board and told us a little bit more about what was going on in the atmosphere. The Big One said, "AFTER JUPITER IS OVER   TOMORROW   10 DAYS JULY 30TH VERY IMPORTANT THIS DATE   10 DAYS AFTER JUPITER 10 PARTS HIT JUPITER BY TOMORROW   JUPITER TIME FOR YOU TO MANIFEST NOW WHATEVER YOU WANT THE MOST   YOU WILL SOON SEE." At the time I heard this, I didn't even research this event with Jupiter. However, while writing this book, I looked into the July date and confirmed that Comet Shoemaker-Levy 9, which broke up and in fact, impacted Jupiter, scarred the planet's upper atmosphere. The Big One said it would hit on the 19th of July. This date has been associated as one of the days of impact.

10/6/94 – We were trying to communicate with the Ouija spirits when, Mary Angel, my personal angel, entered the Board and told us that we couldn't communicate tonight because of the energy. She said, "NOT TONIGHT   LOW ENERGY   CANT   AUSTIN (Austin, TX) LOW RIGHT NOW   CLOUDY ENERGY VERY BLOCKED   IT WILL CLEAR SOON   IT IS NOW AT ITS PEAK   CLEAR YOURSELF THIS WEEKEND GET OUT OF AUSTIN   CANT CONTROL WHEN OTHERS RELEASE."

Apparently, many people within the city of Austin were releasing their own internal issues and problems, which energetically clouded up the electromagnetic frequency used to communicate by the spirits.

1/8/95 – During the middle of a conversation with one of the spirit guides, we were informed about another cloud that was interfering with spiritual development. The Spirit said, "YOU NEED TO LEAVE TOWN   LET THIS CLOUD MOVE ON."

10/1/97 – Starm, an ethereal guide, came in and told us, "TONIGHT THE ENERGY IS THICK   DO THIS 10 12 97." It was explained that the energy was thick in the air. During this session we were fortunate enough to still receive a message, but the message was only a few sentences and not the usual four to five pages filled with communication. Yet, the message that did come through was coherent.

11/23/97 – Starm came in again to communicate briefly after telling us, "THE EARTH IS OUT OF BALANCE RIGHT NOW," which ended the communication for that session.

4/14/13 - I had set aside two days with Victoria, another Ouija Board Operator, to leave the hustle and bustle of the greater Los Angeles area and escape to the quiet and calm environment of Palm Springs for relaxation and Ouija. Wrong! No sooner than arriving there, we found ourselves in a sandstorm that was to last for several days. The sandstorm was so tumultuous, it affected Ouija's ability to communicate. Mostly gibberish came through until they could spell and tell us that they were "BLOCKED" by the sandstorm.

5/7/13 – Victoria and I had opened a session at her house. The planchette's movement felt unusually heavy and moved slowly around the Board. Very unlike how it typically works with Victoria and me. After some gibberish, the Sun was able to inform us that the approaching new moon solar eclipse nearing in two days affected them. They said, "I TRY   MOON IS SLOW AND EVEN SUN TOO." Supposedly, that eclipse was three times stronger than most eclipses.

Your Spiritual Practice

As you must understand by now, from what you have read about using this tool, the Ouija Board, I only suggest it is used in a proactively, positive manner within a positive context for beneficial development. Given the type of expansive communication you will embark upon while using this tool, I highly recommend that you only use this tool if you are engaging in a spiritual practice outside of the Ouija session.

This entails a spiritual practice that supports your internal growth and understanding about life and your relationship within it and within the world. This practice should encompass developing your intuition, a dialogue with your thoughts and with the guiding and protecting energy around you. You may find this within a religion, within a theosophy or philosophy, a mystery school practice, within meditation groups or within movement meditation or yogic postures. Where you can find your practice is endless. The main component that must be included within this spiritual practice is the time for reflective thinking in relationship to the deepening you are experiencing as you are pursuing your practice.

I encourage you, the reader, to start a practice of journaling. Incorporate journaling into your current spiritual practice or the one you will soon be practicing while you are pursuing your Ouija Board communications. Journaling about the session, post session, will allow you to find ways to incorporate the information and a means to determine if it's accurate for you! Just because the message coming through comes from an unseen energy, that many of us attribute to being an All-Knowing presence, does not make it smarter, better or more intelligent than you, for its applications within your life. Warning: never assume that any message coming through the Board is better for your life than what you would determine for yourself. Take the information in, but mull it around inside and discuss it with other people too. Never blindly do anything the Board would tell you to do.

I am suggesting that you open your receptive center to hear the message you receive through Ouija communications, but that you retreat within the knowledge of yourself to decode the truth within the messages. Ouija messages are not always accurate or directly related to your life's path, just like all other forms of psychic, intuitive and mediumistic readings you may have received previously along your path. Remember, Ouija is just a tool. It is just a means for accessing deeper concepts, thoughts and suggestions. However, even with the best of the best messages coming through, YOU ARE THE ONLY ONE who can decipher their application within your life. You are the keeper of the door. You can open it and close it when you choose. This is knowing your own power and your ability to exercise it.

It at any time, you receive a message or communication that makes you uncomfortable, immediately stop the session and close the portal. It's important that you stay in the management position during these sessions. Knowing your own intuition and voice from out of your regular and consistent practice will help you traverse this path with the Ouija spirits in a wise manner.

Yes, I do believe and know from my own experiences that profoundly incredible, mind-blowing, life-changing messages from a session can and will happen. I also know that messages that are from lower energetic vibrations can and will come through, dependent upon your own personal level of spiritual development outside of your Ouija Board practice.

Along these lines, I have said in public, via the radio or other recorded shows, that I do not recommend the practice of doing Ouija by yourself. I stand by this for all new Ouija Board Operators. I repeat, do not use the Ouija Board by yourself when you are developing your work with this tool. This is a tool that can promote obsession and dependence upon the communication that flows. Plus, when you have a partner present with you, you benefit from the value of sharing the unfolding of the sessions with another person as a witness and to extract the truth.

One of the best parts to a Ouija session is the afterwards part, when you end the session and take time to discuss the messages with your partner and the other participants in the room. Reviewing the session through discourse with others is the ultimate way to continue your personal growth through the process of reflection that I mentioned earlier, and a path to maintain a safe and effective relationship with the spirit friends. You are in the physical world of energy to learn and to grow here, not to rely on others from the Beyond to do it for you. It is wonderful to have assistance from the spirit world, but you must always remain grounded within the physical world in which you live. Earth is a school for human beings to re-learn about their greatness and to express this empowerment within the world, while discovering love within their path and within others along their way. You can only do this in the human form when you stay grounded and rely on your fellow humans.

Chapter 5 - Going Public

THE RIGHT PATH HAS MANY BRANCHES
- *The Higher Self*

Coming out of the Closet

Over the early childhood years, I struggled with the secrecy I found myself coveting around my amazing Ouija Board sessions. As you can imagine, it was a very unpopular topic to discuss, as the poor Ouija Board had received mostly negative connotations about it over the most recent decades, during the years that I was learning to use it. I found that it was not a normal topic of conversation and most people, when the subject was broached, had a negative response about it. I heard the gamut of negative adjectives and even expletives about it. The reaction to it was often so extreme that I found it really wasn't worth discussing or sharing with others any of my incredible experiences and information learned from using this tool.

So, in the closet I was, during much of my early, younger years about using this device, and it truly wasn't until my college years that I brought it out into the light and talked more openly about my experiences with the Board. Probably because the formative college years were conducive to learning, exploring and trying new things, so judgment wasn't as harsh and quite frankly, I really didn't care about any judgment at that time. I was still using the Board in a novel manner, yet first-handedly learning much about the existence of the afterlife. This information was exciting and stimulating to a mind already expanding in all sorts of new information I was absorbing within my studies in psychology and through the collegiate environment itself. So, exploring and sharing my Ouija adventures made perfectly good sense during the college years. It was the right type of environment that could handle my "different" means and places for exploration.

When I was out working within my career as an art psychotherapist and licensed professional counselor, I knew I had a code of ethics and professional standing to uphold. I was always thinking I could lose credibility and possibly contracts, clients and even a license or two if I was somehow reported as being so far out there in another's eyes because of my association with the so called demonic Ouija tool. So, I kept my Ouija experiences under wrap, all the while I was actively pursuing and providing past life regressions in my private practice, attending séances and ghost haunting investigations and UFO night watches. Those things seemed "more normal" to others, whereas my Ouija encounters did not.

Strangely, I bought into this and continued to hide my Ouija escapades. However, along the way, there were always close friends and colleagues with whom I did share this part of my life and found myself doing Ouija sessions with many of them. After most people got over their initial mostly negative response to it and after recounting their only experiences with it at a childhood slumber party, they were receptive not because of the Ouija Board, but because of the enlightening and profound experiences I shared with them that I had with the other side. I must mention here that my closer friends throughout my life have been eclectic, more open and often very artistic and inquisitive. So, knowing and trusting me, they were ready to dive in.

Interesting though, there was a subgroup of people with whom I more consistently opened up about my Ouija experiences. After all, I was working in the field of psychology, along with various health providers, healers and counselors, and their openness and their fascination with my use of this tool was surprising well received over all. When I was a practicing therapist, I was using the Ouija Board with the intentions for spiritual growth. With the days of it being used as a novelty gone now, I was getting into some incredibly provocative material.

My closest mental health colleagues and confidents understood this and our sessions deepened in the most fascinating of ways. Backed by our clinical trainings and experiences with helping our clients navigate their psyches, we felt prepared to traverse and navigate the world of the Beyond. With the help of the Board, we began to explore even deeper areas of our psyches, our Higher Selves, experiences with our clients and quandaries about suicide and multiple personality disorders to name a few. We were seeing and experiencing the traumatic stories of our clients, but now we could explore the fabulous facets of the human mind and consciousness at deeply profound levels with the help of our spirit friends, our angels, various entities and other helpers we met through the portal of the Ouija Board.

And Into the Light

The entities with whom we spoke became our spirit friends. We developed a consistency with the information they shared with us. We were beginning to trust them as you would come to trust any other person within your life. The big difference is that they were unseen at that time and often they had never been incarnated within the physical world. We were learning so much that we were personally growing by leaps and bounds and further expanding our spiritual understandings through our conversations with them.

Protection was the most important mechanism I had in place any and every time we touched the Board and opened the channel of communication with them. I understood from prior experiences and from some of the other negative stories I had heard about the Ouija over the years, to have clear and concise intentions when approaching the Board and to take an inventory of our own feeling states, as well, when operating the Board.

I also found myself serving as a guide, if you will, for people who did the Ouija with me or were a part of the sessions. I would instruct about the use of this tool, teaching a participant how to approach a session, how to open oneself to the messages and how to interact with the other side. Basically, I was serving as the gatekeeper between the unseen and the seen. I realized that I was serving as both the keeper of this portal and the guide to navigating the other side. It was a fascinating role and somebody had to do it. I was obliged and honored.

Once I found myself working within the high-tech wireless industry, I went underground again with my Ouija work. My work with the Board lessened, as I worked long hours at building my company and filling my mind with left brain thinking and technical specifications. There were some friends during this time who attempted to work the Board with me, but mostly, the results and communication were sparse and incoherent. There was not a main staple of people with whom I could take and make the time to practice the Board enough times and with consistency to help develop a connection to the other side. I began to think that it was not the right timing within my life to do this work regularly as I had earlier in life been able to do. Instead, I focused on journaling as my means of connecting with my spirit friends and at this time, I mostly spoke to Mary Angel, either out loud or in my journaling. They never left me, just gave me the space to develop my work within my left-brain. This stagnant and sparse period with the Ouija lasted for about five years.

However, during this stagnant time, I still had very engaging Ouija Board sessions every now and then with one of my brothers, the one who originally was involved with my Wilma Jean encounter, every time he came for a visit to see me. I looked forward to his visits, as we have always been able to operate the Ouija Board with great results, allowing coherent and interesting communication.

Along the way, I met other friends who were interested in what I was doing with the Ouija Board. I shared with select individuals how I used the Board as a tool for spiritual growth. Pretty much everyone whose interest with the Board turned into a fascination with the Board and desire to work the Board with me, all had their introduction to the Ouija Board in childhood.

I had families, girl friends, boy friends, colleagues and acquaintances engage with the Board and me. Not everyone worked as an Ouija Operator with me, only a few have over the years. That was perfectly fine by many of the people, as they were just as happy sitting in on a session and receiving messages.

I guess with age comes an attitude of "I don't care what you think!" As I stepped into my forties, I realized that I couldn't hide my work with my spirit friends anymore, and as I came to this realization, I let the proverbial cat out of the bag. This is code for, I placed all of my Ouija Boards out in my homes, decorating the main rooms, the living room and dining area. Given Ouija's past with speaking with the dead, what a fitting placement. Ouija was right at home within the rooms of my "living" space.

Often I was asked by a curious friend or two to "do the Ouija" when I didn't have a Ouija Board on hand. Yes, I have been known to travel with one, but no Board, no worries, "Do we have cardboard or a paper sack on hand?" During these occasions, I would fashion a Ouija Board onto a paper sack or other disposable surface with a marker, find a double old fashion glass or my favorite, the Pyrex dish, to serve as the planchette and away we would go. Voila, instant Ouija! If the occasion deemed right, the spirits could instantly communicate no matter where I was, any time and with any group. When I felt that the situation at hand called for spirit communication, I would just create a Ouija Board.

All who heard the experiences and accounts were at least curious on some level. With their curiosity, came their questions, addressing their how's and why's to this unusual form of communication. These sincere questions and desire to "try" the Ouija Board helped ease me into becoming comfortably open to share about my long time use of Ouija and my long time relationships with the spirit friends from Beyond.

The veil was lifting. A new era was dawning.

Chapter 6 - The Deceased

YOU ALREADY KNOW WHAT TO DO
YOU HOLD ALL THE ANSWERS
-*The Sun*

Spirits & Ghosts

When I first began my work on the Ouija Board, I truly thought that Ouija could only be used to talk to the dead, including the spirits of deceased loved ones and spirits that may be stuck, you know, the ones who were responsible for creating ghostly apparitions and hauntings. Not exactly true! Over the years I have learned that not only can we speak with the deceased, we can communicate with many other different consciousness that exists in its varying forms, such as animals that are both alive and dead, people in comas, unborn fetuses, angels, guides, ethereal beings and our Higher Self.

As I discuss more about spirit and ghosts in this chapter, I'd like to explain what I believe to be the difference between the two. Both are similar in that they are the energetic extension of deceased human beings, including deceased animals. However, they differ in their motivation and reasons for being around.

A deceased person remains in his spirit form when he has business to tend to with his loved ones. Business includes, staying on as a spirit guardian for the family or maybe just for a single member of the family to help any or all of them grow. This spirit may have a message to communicate or a period of time to stay around, while the mourners are learning to cope with their loss. The spirit has intentions to share his love and support, thus remains around the family or a person to assist.

On the other hand, I have learned that a deceased person's spirit can become "stuck" on the other side when an agenda of her past personality consumed her presence when she died and into the after life. This overwhelming agenda can cause the creation of a ghostly apparition or haunting. Being extremely attached to her life or another person, the spirit can carry this attachment into the spirit realm with her unfinished business. This spirit hangs around haunting a space until the business or message is heard. This is when a place will be haunted with the same footsteps walking the floor, the same wailing cries from the attic or the same passing of a misty form from one room to another, oblivious to any walls or people.

A devastating, sudden and tragic death can knock a person into an unawareness of "being" dead when they cross over. Couple this unawareness with a strong emotion, such as anger, from the recent personality, the spirit can become stuck while not shedding the personality and strong emotion. Instead he remains stuck in a repetitious cycle of reenacting the strong emotion. When a ghost is finally aware of live people being around and that it is actually dead, that's when there is real hope for the ghost to release itself from its earthbound bondage of repetitious hell.

Spirits

As I mentioned earlier in this book, my very first Ouija experience was a communication session with the spirit of the deceased sister of the Johnson girls' who lived down the street from my family and me. The impact of this first session was so profound, I just knew that I had to experience and learn more about communicating with our deceased relatives and various other spirits. I wanted to communicate with any and all that were out there, those who were still around us and had not moved on to a new incarnation.

I have learned that once a person dies, their spirit can and often will stay around us in an ethereal existence. Depending upon the karmic contract* we have with this other person. Learning continues even when the other person leaves her body and enters into the ethereal realms. This person may stay around to serve as a guardian to her loved ones, to help comfort the survivor's feelings of loss, to give a message that she feels compelled to give and to share insights. Sometimes a spirit becomes stuck and unable to move on because of the strong pull she receives from the survivors' pain with the acceptance of her death and their loss.

Wilma Jean

Although, I have spoken with many spirits of the deceased, I have a warm place in my heart for a bygone, spirit friend, Wilma Jean whom we eventually helped release into the light. There is always a time and season for everything, including the relationships with our spirit friends, who too must move on, into their next level of soul evolution. Before I lay this story to rest, I must share with you my relationship with Wilma Jean.

When Wilma Jean was alive, she existed as an African-American slave in the south. She groveled in the cotton fields her entire life of 35 years. She was self-taught in basic reading and writing and came through the Board as an extremely positive and happy spirit. Her life was cut short when the slave owner murdered her. Given her circumstances, she was never bitter and offered many messages of support to all who interacted with her through the Board. Wilma often served as an escort, helping other spirits come through the Board and communicate. She would help them learn to interact via the planchette and made certain any negative influences would not come through. She was one of my first "bouncers" on the other side. Our relationship lasted for about a decade when I realized that she was not moving on into the light nor was she like Mary, my angel, who left her humanly existence to become one of the celestial* beings. With a better understanding of how our interaction "could" be keeping her earth bound, I questioned the longevity of this relationship. After all, she had existed on the other side for about 150 years since she was murdered. I decided we needed to have a talk about the light and to finally merge with it.

Around this time, I had been studying hypnosis and regression therapy under the tutelage of Dr. Coletta Long. I spent a year undergoing past life regressions as a client of Dr. Long's, which then turned into two years, as I was accepted into her Inner Guidance Center clinical program for clinicians only and trained to become a past life therapist. During my personal past life recalls I first-handedly learned much about what happens in between incarnations. This information so happened to correspond exactly with my Ouija Board friends' portrayal of the other side. This was an exciting time, because not only was I remembering my past lives, I was learning how to directly work with the light within and without during the recall of these distant memories for purposes of healing trapped and blocked somatic and emotional energy. I also learned that in between lives, a soul could get lost and forget his way back into the light. I encountered many lost souls during my own regression memories and during the regressions of my clients when they were in between lives.

The light within is truly the energetic makeup of our souls and the power that our spirit uses to teleport, to transmute and to transcend any fear within us that ultimately causes blocks and barriers to our true essence. When we can't locate or can't see the light, either within ourselves or outside ourselves, while passing over to the other side, we will enter a state of feeling lost from our essence. We don't necessarily turn into negative and dark energy because we can't locate the light, but the effect of not going into the light and not merging back with our source, will cause souls to become lost from returning to their essence. These souls are typically unaware of the light and will end up wandering the lower planes of existence and cause the stuck phenomena we call ghosts and hauntings.

Fear is the opposite of love. When we are in the light, we are in the essence of love. When we are unable to find the light, we are in fear. Fear creates darkness, which is just a temporary absence of light. Darkness does not equate to negativity, although many religions would like us to believe this. Being in the light is being illuminated and enlightened. To have knowledge, we must awaken to the light. Being in the dark means we just don't know. When we don't know something, we can fall into the trap of becoming fearful of that which we don't know, we don't understand and we can't experience.

Wilma Jean's experience on the other side is an example how a spirit can die and not find the light. Yet, fortunately, she did not become fearful. That is what I find the most endearing about Wilma. She existed in this in between space as a soul and contently accepted her lot. She didn't appear lost or afraid. She observed life as it changed within our realm. Wilma did want to know if this was all there was that she experienced from her recent life recall when we conversed about her existence on the other side. She found herself interacting with other souls who also had not gone into the light. They weren't negative or demonic as many would want to label them. They just existed within the world of their recent life personalities, knowing they were dead, but not knowing that they should move into a light and not knowing that they were to transmute that past personality, back into the light of their essence. What light, they wondered?

Wilma Jean was never aware of this all-providing light. She came to us over the Board because she was attracted to a light that turned out to be our light, the light we created when we placed our finger tips on the planchette and intended our communication with the other side. My understanding from the other side is that this intention and connection between the people using the Ouija Board creates a light, a portal of light, in which many are attracted. This is like a moth to the flame. Without illumination, in a space absent of light, this new light creates quite an attraction on the other side. This light attracts all moths, meaning, all wandering spirits!

Very Important!

Now, you can begin to understand why using the Ouija Board and opening this portal to the other side can foreseeably get one into trouble. When you turn the light on, anyone and everyone can show up. This speaks volumes for establishing boundaries with the other side by tuning your intentions to a frequency of positive gain for both parties. This in turn sets the atmosphere, the vibration of the portal, to keep out lower vibrations from entering. Only vibrations that match the keepers of the portal (you!) can enter.

When I met Wilma Jean, I didn't understand all of the inner workings of this portal and was still in my infancy working with the light within, in my own life. Fortunately, I was growing in my understanding that I could use the power of my mind to visualize myself blanketed in a protective light. Since I was majoring in psychology at the time I met Wilma Jean, I was learning about this concept by reading various text books and by being involved with various research studies. As easily as I attracted Wilma Jean to my

Ouija Board, I could have attracted anyone that was out there wandering around. I wasn't ready in spiritual understanding to even ask to communicate with my angels and guides. I was only focused on talking to dead people. After all, that was how the Ouija Board was marketed, to speak with the dead. However, with whom I communicated over the Board shifted as my spiritual awareness grew and I began studying spiritual practices.

One of my most memorable spirit communication sessions ever, which was earth shattering and transformational for all who were present, was the college session when we communicated with Lindsey's deceased sister while being blindfolded. What came through was the most profoundly moving message that created a lasting memory of heartfelt closure and healing to a death.

To this day, friends and acquaintances often come to my sessions, requesting a message from a dear loved one who has passed on. Not always will the requested love one provide a message, nor are they always capable of doing so at that time. There are a few different reasons why they may not communicate. One reason is that they are not ready to communicate because they are still healing from their passing and not in the vicinity or even strong enough to communicate through the portal. Another reason, quite possibly the person requesting the loved one to speak to her is really not ready to hear or receive any message from the deceased. Yet another reason, the spirit has moved on into another incarnation already or could also be "busy" working in their new role on the other side. Yes, we do continue to learn, grow and evolve when we leave behind our physical, human experience.

The sessions containing loved ones' messages are often quite touching experiences, as both the deceased participant and the live participant get to communicate in a tangible way as if they are engaged in a normal, everyday conversation again. When I work the Board, I speak to the spirits with a respect as I would anyone else in the room that is present. They are a part of the conversation and I direct both the other operator and myself to keep our fingers resting on the planchette at all times even when we are having side-related conversations with any other participants at that session. In this manner, the spirits can interact in our conversations as anyone else could that is present. The planchette is their necessary link, allowing them to interact within our world. When the planchette moves, it's important to stop all talk and allow the spelling, even if someone is in mid sentence. Again, it's about showing respect for the communication that transpires.

For example, on July 24, 2013, Bev wanted to be in communication with a couple of deceased family members. She wanted to speak with her father and hear from her sister. Her sister was currently unable to communicate as she was still healing on the other side from her terrible bout with substance abuse that ultimately led to her death. Her deceased father came through, sharing fatherly thoughts of encouragement and care for Bev. He encouraged her to live her life. Bev attended the session as a participant only, without her hands touching the planchette at any given time, while her father spelled out messages to her:

I AM ALAWYS [*sic*] WITH YOU   PROTECTING YOU THE BEST I CAN KEEP THE FAITH   YOU CAN DO ANYTHING YOU WANT TO JUST HAVE TO BELIEVE   YOU NEED TO BELIEVE IN YOURSELF AND IT WILL SHOW   START LIVING IN THE MOMENT   VISUALIZE YOUR LIFE AS YOU WANT IT   REMEMBER YOU CAN ONLY CHANGE YOURSELF   WE ALL NEED TO LOOK AT OURSELF AND WHAT DO I NEED TO WORK ON   LOVE YOU WITH ALL MY HEART

While Bev's father was delivering this message, a true back and forth conversation transpired. The planchette would move and spell, then stop or swirl around the Board, waiting for the next question or statement Bev inquired and stated. In order to have this type of conversation, I encourage Bev to go into her heart, feel his words and speak to him from this space as if he was right there with us in person again. It made the communication real, while a heart-warming conversation ensued. I have learned that the energies on the other side have an easier time communicating with us when we settle into a communicative space that feels natural and comfortable for us. All the while we are conversing with everyone present (the alive and the disembodied), I maintain one hand on the planchette, the other hand holding a pen and writing and serve as the mediator to deepen the experience for both sides of the communicating parties. Talk about multi-tasking!

Ghosts & Spirit Releasement

I have encountered ghosts on the Board, but not as often as I do spirits and other ethereal beings on the Board. Ghosts come through on the Board three different ways in my experience. They come through because I have been in a place where they inhabit and they made their presence noticeable. This is when I have literally seen their apparition or experienced them through my senses. At other times, I have requested them to come forward and communicate as a response to investigating poltergeist activity in a house. The only other way they have come through the Board is when they have stumbled upon a session and often come through dazed and unaware of their death. This has always been quite fascinating to witness, as it is reminiscent of the bleed-through you would get on a circuit board telephone of yesteryear. It's like talking to one person over the phone and all of a sudden, another person starts talking and now you have a new person on your line. This is what they used to call having your lines crossed or entering a party line. The experience of this bleed-though on the Board is quite similar. The confused and stuck ghost comes across a light, which is the energy of our communication between us and our spirit friends on the other side, and the confused ghost jumps on this energy and uses it for its communication. Now, seemingly out of nowhere, I have a dazed and confused ghost entering an on-going conversation and saying unrelated things and inquiring where they are.

Samuel

The experience with Samuel is a good example of how a trapped ghost will communicate and can continue communicating even after you have left the vicinity where communication was originally opened. It was August 14, 1995 and I was invited into a home located on Francis E. Warren Air Force Base in Cheyenne, Wyoming that had poltergeist type activity within it, such as, items getting moved from one place to another, lights going on and off on their own, a bread warmer that would open on its own and other similar activities. Now, this Air Force Base has a long and unique history as first being established in 1867 by the US Calvary as a military facility to protect the workers building the Union Pacific Railroad in Wyoming against attacks by Indians before becoming a Base to the Air Force in 1949. The couple that lived there said they heard noises coming from the attic often that left them feeling creeped-out. So, I decided the four of us, my Ouija partner, the wife who lived there, a friend and I would get right down to business as we entered the attic for our communication.

No sooner than we opened the session, a ghost named Samuel came through. He claimed he was a seventeen-year-old servant boy who lived in the house's attic with his 3-year-old dog named Queen. He persistently and repeatedly told us that he was alive. He admitted to opening the bread warmer to remind the occupants that he is here and that there are many others who stay in the house too.

As we spoke with him and heard his story spell out across the Board, it became apparent that his consciousness was moving in and out of realities. It was as if he was living within two dimensions, one where we were and the other of his past. He interrupted the story he was telling us with a bleed-through-like action story. He said:

I FIGHT OFFICER   I WILL GET HIM   I WILL WAIT FOR HIM   I WILL NOT HURT YOU   I WILL HELP PROTECT WHEN HOME

He told us that his dog was kicked and knifed by someone, which led us to believe it was the Officer he mentioned above because after he told us about his dog, he interrupted himself with the dialogue aforementioned. At this point in the conversation, I advised him that there is no one he must fight anymore. As I was attempting to bring him back into our present reality that he was dead and stuck within a past event involving an officer and his dog, he said:

SLEEP NOW   PLEASE GO NOW   YOU GO   GOOD BYE   LEAVE ME ALONE   NOW GO   LEAVE NOW   GO   GO

As he was spelling this, the planchette moved with increased speed and erratic movements from on letter to the next. I could feel the angry an intense energy within the planchette's movement and what he was spelling. At this point, I decided it best to end this session since he was verbally fighting us. We closed the session. The very next day, I heard from the occupant of the house that the grandmother's clock hanging on a wall not too far away from the bread warmer had somehow detached from the wall and fell to the floor.

Very Important!

Now, the story doesn't end there. This is where I place another WARNING sign. Understand when communication is opened through the portal of a Talking Board, you may not be able to close the communication if you don't find an agreeable ending with the spirit or ghost when you end a session. With Samuel, we didn't have that. We ended the session with him expressing anger and shutting us out. You

must learn and know what to do if this ever happens in a session.
Again, "OUIJA IS NOT FOR THE WEAK OR UNINFORMED," as the Sun,
one of my ethereal spirits with whom I speak, told us in a future
session.

Flash forward six days from our original contact and
communication with Samuel. We opened the Board to speak with my
Angel named Mary and she said the following:

NOT TONIGHT   DARKNESS IS HERE

Then Samuel jumped into the conversation and said:

GET OUT OF MY SPACE

I told Samuel that we were not in his space anymore; he tried to argue
that we still were. I then asked Mary Angel to step in and remove him
from the Board's portal. She agreed to and wrapped Samuel in a cloak
of light and he actually replied to this gesture with a thanks.

Mary Angel then told us:

WATCH OUT FOR SAMUEL   POWERFUL ATTRACTION   YOU [*sic*]
BRIGHT LIGHT

I learned that was Mary Angel's reminder to always call upon our
spirit helpers on the other side to serve as protectors of our portal and
communications when an errant spirit or ghost jumps into the
communication at hand. We should always have them involved when

we open communication with a ghost, and for that matter, any spirit or entity we invite to communicate with us.

If the communication with a spirit ever becomes demeaning, derogatory, angry or abusive in any way, you immediately stop the session. State out loud a prayer to close the session and send white light to the communication you just shut down. Also state out loud that you and the other participants remain surrounded in this protective light. Request that your spirit friends cloak the errant spirit or ghost in light so that he too may find his way back into the light. The important lesson is to always invite your spirit helpers to all sessions and do not engage with any entity that is negative in any way. Remember, your responsibility is to manage the session and portal you opened.

Tom McEachrun

This story is an example of a deceased person who came through the Board to communicate after I had been in the vicinity of where his energy was lingering and had not moved on into the light at that time.

During my brother's visit with me in San Clemente, California we decided to pull the Board out and give it a spin on September 16, 2001. Again, this is the brother who operates the Ouija Board with me quite well. No sooner than we started the session, it began spelling the following:

MCKEACHRUN TOM   TOM WATER DIE RAINED   JANE KNEW ME
MY NAME IS TOM   JANE PEOPLE SIT ON ME   LOOK AT BEACH 4
TOM   REMEMBER ME   LOOK 4 ME BY THE SHOWER   SIT ON ME
TRAIPD [*sic*]   THERE NOW   FEEL MY NAME   THE TRACKS R
[*sic*]LOUD

Earlier that day, my brother, a friend and I were down at the beach enjoying the day playing in the water and sand. At that time, I lived about a block away from the state beach park located in San Clemente. At this park, above the ocean, the city had placed a few concrete benches. Never had I sat on them or even noticed that they were inscribed with people's names and sayings. When Tom spelled out, "PEOPLE SIT ON ME," we decided to go visit the park and benches the next day. Sure enough, there is one bench located there, inscribed with: "Tom McEachrun, One with the Sea." A little eerie to me because he indicted he was trapped there and could hear the loudness of the trains on the tracks. Yes, there are train tracks about 50 yards away from the location of the benches and trains go by continually all day, every day. He also wanted us to look for him. No thank you!

I never spoke with Tom again, but I was a little creeped-out to go down to the beach for my early morning run around 5:30, as I had been doing for some time. I decided to run through the neighborhood instead. I know that Tom would have come through the Board again if he needed to. I do believe that he has finally moved on and has gone into the light.

Hector

This story is an example of a deceased person who stumbles upon the Board's open portal as we are operating it. He comes through confused to where he is. It's as if his spirit has been alone for many, many years, trapped in darkness. In reality, he had been and the story doesn't end there. The unfolding of the events of this session alleviates Hector's confusion and assists him through the process of releasing his spirit into the light.

Again, it was during another visit by my infamous brother, but this time his wife accompanied him and they were visiting me in the Palm Springs area. On July 9, 2011, we sat down for a session in which my brother and I were operating the Board. We were inquiring for personal messages from our guides when in jumps a confused, deceased person who says the following to us:

82975 AVE REQUA   HECTOR   DO U [*sic*] KNOW ME   I AM A TRAP LOOK AT ME AT 82975 REQUA   29 YEARS   FREE ME   WHERE ARE U   I AM AT 82975   INDIO   HELP FREE ME   U R [*sic*] TALKING TO ME   U ARE THE ONLY 1 WHO HAS THE STRENGTH   HECTOR LOCATE 82975   PROVIDE HELP   FREE HIM   I AM HERE   HELP

PLEASE HELP   WHERE AM I   TELL ME WHERE AM I   82975 REQUA

AVE   TELL ME WHERE I AM AT

I then called upon my angel, Mary Angel, to step in and assist

Hector. I asked Hector if he could see Mary and if he understood that

Mary would help him. He then said the following:

I HAVE KNOWN MARY FOR LONG TIME   TELL ME WHERE I AM AT

MARY DOESN'T KNOW   PLEASE TELL ME   MARY WOULD U [*sic*]

PLEASE HELP   WHERE AM I   PLEASE FRIEND OF MARY PLEASE

BEEN HERE FOR 75 Y [*sic*]

Hector was quickly spelling on the Board at this time, repeating the

same questions over and over again, asking where he is. With Mary

Angel available and Hector being able to see her, I asked her to show

him the light. At this point, I am mostly doing the talking and once in

awhile the Board moves to yes or no during my verbal directions to

Mary to show Hector the light and request that Hector follow Mary

into the light.

Hector then says the following as he finally confirms that he is

going with Mary into the light:

CANT CANT CANT   WHERE   WHERE [*sic*] NAME   82975 WHERE   I

AM HAPPY 2 KNOW NAME OF 82975   GOING WITH MARY

At the conclusion of releasing Hector into the light with Mary

guiding him there, we looked up the address on the Internet that

109

Hector frantically provided. Sure enough we found it on a map. The next day, all of us drove over there together and discovered that the address is associated with a funeral home. Interestingly, the property does not have a name out front that indicates it's a funeral home; that signage is on the side of the building. However, the address 82975 is big and bold on the front of the building. This is what Hector saw all of the seventy-five years he had been in that space. From his message, it sounds like he died at the age of twenty-nine.

During the session it was clear to me that all of the details surrounding his death were not important. It would have been selfish of us to inquire to any more details for our own curiosity. What was important to him was what he was repeatedly asking and stating. He did not know where he was and this fixation is what confused him all of these years and kept him from going into the light. Spirit releasement is about helping those who are stuck, by helping them find peace and solace within and then in turn, they can open to the light and go there.

Theresa & Styrmy

This next story takes place in Cabo San Lucas, Mexico while I was on a weeklong golf trip with a friend there. First I must say that I was not going to Mexico to speak or experience the dead nor did I bring a

Ouija Board with me to do so. There are times when I do travel with a Board, knowing that there will be a circumstance that requires investigation or knowing that I will be with another Ouija Board Operator and we will make the time to have a session. In the case of this trip, unbeknownst to me, my friend Jenny brought her small Ouija Board that fits nicely in a suitcase and comes with a glow-in-the-dark planchette. By the way, this is the perfect-sized Ouija Board for traveling.

It was the second or third night into the trip. We had made an early evening of it, as we did most evenings since every morning was filled with early morning golf or sightseeing. I awoke in the wee hours of the morning, needing to use the restroom. I got out of my bed and was walking towards the bathroom, which was on the other side of Jenny's bed when all of a sudden, a woman's apparition literally popped up in front of me before I made it to the bathroom. This woman's backside was to me and she was located within eighteen inches from me. I could see her dark hair held up by a comb and her shoulders and back clothed in white briquetted and eyelet trimmed Victorian gown with big, white puffy sleeves hanging over the shoulders.

I screamed out while at the same time flying through the air and landing in Jenny's bed, waking her up and telling her to "look, there's a ghost in here!" Quite dumbfounded, she looked at me and said, "What's the matter? You like ghosts." I told her that I don't like them when they come out of the blue and pop up in front of me without being invited. Jenny, still not affected by what just happened, mockingly gets out of bed, swinging her arms through the air as if clearing the space of the ghost, telling me that there is nothing here now and to go back to bed.

Shocked and in recovery mode from a near heart attack brought on by that unexpected visitor, I go back to my bed, flip on the lamp between our beds and notice a little glow-in-the-dark planchette, placed there and pointing towards my bed. Let's see, I wonder who put that there? I told Jenny that by placing a planchette, pointing at me, it's like opening the portal to the other side and yelling, "Contact Karen, 1-800-OUIJA-4U!" This was the first time I was even aware that she had brought her Ouija Board with her on this trip, let alone set out the planchette, pointing in my direction. Yikes!

As I said before, Ouija is not a game and we must take care to only work with it when we are prepared to do so and our intentions are in the right space. What seemed like a harmless little prank, to purposely place the planchette there without my knowledge, really turned out to be an opening to the other side. I believe this happened because of the many years I have been operating the Ouija Board, I've created a direct connection with the other side that can easily be accessed when the tools of communication are placed with these intentions. I also understand that since I know that I am protected and safe while I do this work, nothing can enter this portal that has malicious and mischievous intent regardless of who placed that planchette there.

When morning finally came and we headed to the resort's dining room for breakfast, I told Jenny I would inquire about any reports of ghosts on their property from the staff or visitors. I inquired about "fantasmas" in my best-broken attempts at speaking in Spanish to our waiter. Turns out he spoke English quite well, so we were able to have a decent and understandable conversation about ghosts. He was reticent at first to answer my questions about any reports of ghosts on the property, but after we were at his table for some time and I inquired with a few more questions, he opened up.

Our waiter told us that there have been several reports of a young child who runs through the dining room early in the mornings when they come into the room and are readying the tables with place settings. (Note: This is a resort that only caters to adults or children that are at least 16 or older, if accompanied by an adult.) This child who appears to be a young girl, runs through the dining room and often knocks dishes from the tables. The waiter continued to tell us that they have not heard of this happening for a few months, but this morning, there was a report of having seen this young girl again! The waiter said that my questions about ghosts were eerie since this just happened this morning.

Now, we were talking and definitely committed to discussing their ghostly encounters. Next, I inquired if anyone has seen an adult ghost anywhere on this property. He said, "Well, as a matter of fact, people see a beautiful woman in a long white dress, walking the beach late at night." He proceeded to tell me that's when someone may call out to her thinking she is a guest to see if she needs anything, and no sooner than they spoke their words, she quickly disappears. (Note: This is an all-inclusive beach resort, where the staff is constantly inquiring if you need anything.)

That was when I told him that I saw what I believed to be this woman in my room right over there, as I pointed towards our room, early that same morning. His mouth opened and his face displayed a look of slight shock and fear. I told him not to worry, but that I will attempt to communicate to this apparition and will let him know what we discover. I'm sure that sounded crazy to him, but I felt the need to relieve him of any fear because after all, we weren't feeling fearful and I just had a direct run in with this apparition.

That afternoon, after our days' events, my friend and I brought out her Ouija Board and attempted to make contact with whomever was in our room the night before. In Spanish the Board spelled:

ME ASUSTASTE (which is Spanish for you scared me)

We were both taken aback what this spelled out because first of all, I was scared silly and second of all, it was spelled in Spanish! I said out loud, "Are you kidding me? You scared me!" Then I said it in Spanish, "No, me asustaste!"

I then requested that the spirit friends on the other side assist this being with her communication, but in English, as that would allow the session to flow for us better. Over a couple of sessions, we learned that the name of the apparition that appeared to me in our room was Theresa and that she is also the same woman who walks along the beach at night searching for her daughter. She stumbled into our room because she found the light of the portal (from the Planchette) and came towards it. She was oblivious that she was inside of a room, let alone a building. She was not even aware of people. She was on a mission and that mission being that she finds her daughter, Styrmy. That was why she was scared when we both bumped into each other the night before. She wasn't expecting people and in fact, didn't even know she was dead.

As the story unfolded over a couple of sessions, we learned that her daughter was raped and murdered at the hands of her husband. She was so distraught that she threw herself into the sea only to drown herself. She existed in this hell she created since the late 1800s, walking the vicinity, repeating the same steps and looking for her murdered daughter. I told Theresa that we think we found her daughter and to look for her just South of where we were communicating with her, about one hundred feet away.

When we went down for breakfast the following morning, after having spoken with Theresa about her existence and her lost daughter, Styrmy, the same waiter looked at us with big eyes and said that the staff saw the child run through the dining room again that morning. I then shared that we made communication with the lady apparition and shared what we had learned from her. I told him everything and also said that we told Theresa where to find her daughter, as we believed that this child running through the dining room is her lost daughter. I predicted to the waiter that once they find each other, I said I doubt that they will still see the little girl run through the dining room anymore.

We spoke to Theresa again after breakfast and asked her if she found her daughter. Theresa came through the Board, expressing her happiness for being reunited with her daughter, telling us that Styrmy is now safe. I spoke to Theresa about the love she has for her daughter and how this love transcends all time and always will. I told them that now they are both safe and together again. I asked our spirit friends to help Theresa and Styrmy see and feel the light within and without.

116

Theresa said that she was not letting go of Styrmy ever again nor would she leave this place where they existed together. I gave Theresa the speech about the importance of going into the light, but she would not have anything to do with it. Although she was thankful to have our help to reunite with her daughter, she chose to stay in her space. All of this was communicated through the Board.

At this stand still, I knew that no one could ever force anyone or anything into the light. Remember, everyone has free will. All I could do was send her positive wishes, requests to our spirit friends to watch over her and help her and her daughter in time. So, I really thought this would be the end of the story, but wait; it doesn't end there in Mexico.

Once back in California on an evening about three months later, when the same friend from the trip was visiting at my house, we decided to communicate with our spirit friends over the Board. Who do you think came through? Yes, it was Theresa and she was chatty and happy. I asked her about going into the light where all of her other loved ones were waiting for her. She still did not want any part of that, but I asked her to at least look up and into the light knowing that she had full capability to do as she wanted. She trusted me, so she looked into the light and commented on how she saw members of her family there. I asked her to consider stepping towards them. She hesitantly

117

agreed to and once she did, the light enveloped her and Styrmy. Mary Angel stepped in to help her as did Theresa's loved ones. Communication continued in a yes and no format until I could feel the energy shift and off she want into the light, telling us how beautiful it was. My friend Jenny inquired just what that was all about and I told her that she just participated in her first spirit releasement session.

Spirits Becoming Earthbound Ghosts

A word of caution when using the Ouija Board; it is not only possible, but it can happen where overly zealous communication with a deceased person, a spirit, can contribute to a spirit becoming attached and earthbound. Basically, the communication can create an attachment for the spirit who already had a propensity to being attached to its recent life and struggled with accepting its death. This newfound communication with the living can fill the gap it feels from its death and the life it left behind. Be very cautious. I will explain further.

Anne King

As I discussed earlier in this book, Anne King was communicating with us quite regularly. It was very easy to call upon her and she was ready, willing and able to come through with clear communication. Not only did she speak to Linda and me over the Board, she would speak to others in the house who we had introduced to using the Ouija Board. One sorority sister in particular, Sandy, became obsessed with speaking to Anne King. In fact, Sandy kept Linda's larger-sized Ouija Board that had been in Linda's family since the sixties, within her room. She and her roommate and other Ouija Operators would work with Sandy on the Board as she communicated with Anne King.

There were reports of items falling off the walls in Sandy's room while they engaged in communication with Anne King. Around this same time, the house mother of the sorority, reported a cowboy hat she had hanging on her bed post as flying around her room at night. The house mother did not know that quite a few of us in the sorority house were using the Ouija Board and frequently communicating with a spirit who was now earning the reputation of creating poltergeist type events. I never witnessed these events, but I had my own experience instead.

It was between classes and Linda and I were in the room we shared at the sorority house. She was sitting in her bed, working on a class assignment. I was lying down in my bed with my back turned towards Linda, resting but fully awake when I felt a hand nudge me on my back as if to ask me an urgent question. I didn't turn to face Linda, instead I said, "What!" Linda said, "What do you want?" At this point I rolled over, now facing her from within my bed and said, "You just touched me, what do you need?" With a puzzled look on her face she told me she didn't touch me nor did she need anything. I told her that I felt a physical hand on my back, giving me an urgent nudge. She said that no one else was in the room and of course, if someone came in, I would have heard this person come in. After all, I wasn't asleep, just resting before another class I had to leave for in about 15 minutes. We both agreed that this was strange, and never said another thing about it.

The next time we had a Ouija session with Anne King, she proceeded to tell us that she was the one who touched me. I told her that was creepy and that this was going too far and that we would not communicate with her anymore if she was going to display herself in physical ways. She obviously did not like what I was saying as she became belligerent and "told off" Linda and me. In my mind, Anne was becoming too much alive and I just knew this was not healthy for her.

At this point, the fun and games and interesting stories started to change. I told Anne that we would speak to her less, she was not allowed to curse at us and that she needed to move on into the light. Again, she didn't want to hear this and started her name calling and cussing again. Linda, Dena and I agreed that Anne King needed to be released from our communications. We told her a few times and then we finally just stopped talking with her. Since we wouldn't talk to her when she got this way, she started communicating more and more with Sandy.

Sandy became obsessed with using the Ouija Board and talking to Anne King. In fact, so obsessed that she went to class less and less. Sandy didn't want me to know this, but others were telling me this. Finally, I went up to her room and told her that she needs to stop this obsession. Give the Ouija Board back to Linda and go to class. I also told Sandy that by talking to Anne all of the time, we are in a sense, holding her back from her own evolution as a soul. I told Sandy that Anne needs to move on, but of course, Sandy told me she would at least slow down with the Board communication. I let Sandy know that the rest of us were done communicating with Anne.

Sincerely hoping Anne King would move into the next plane of existence she was to inhabit, if we left her alone, I stopped all communication with her forever. I rarely brought up her name after I graduated from college and moved on from the sorority house. However, I returned to the Sorority house after being away for about twenty years, when I attended an alumnae function. Deciding to make a visit and see what changes the house has undergone, Linda and I visited the house together that evening. The current sorority sisters who greeted us at the door, happily showed us around. Surprisingly, one of them told us that the ghost of Anne King haunts their house. My mouth literally dropped to the floor and Linda and I just looked at each other. I made an inquisitive type statement, something to the effect that after all of these years, "Anne is still here?" I confided in the college girls that we were the ones who originally communicated with Anne and mistakenly communicated with her for too long. I told them that some day Anne King needs to move on and that it is really best for her, whether or not Anne agrees. To my knowledge and to the publishing date of this book, Anne still walks those halls.

Sharon, Jay & Steven

I was recently invited to a home on Cielo Drive, located in Benedict Canyon of Los Angeles, which is four doors down from the scene of the most gruesome and notorious murders that occurred in 1969. At the end of the drive is where six lives, including an unborn baby, were horrifically taken at the hands of a clan of murderers. I was introduced to the owner of this home because of my work making successful connections via the Ouija Board. The ghosts of Sharon, Jay and Steven, in addition to other entities, haunt this house. The owner believes that his house has not only become a safe haven for the spirits of Sharon,

Jay and Steven, but a portal to the other side where various entities enter.

We decided to first walk through the house and find out what, if anything, our senses would experience. Both of us, my Ouija Board partner and I felt a feeling of nausea go over us when we entered the laundry room located on the bottom floor of this house. Apparently, that was the floor where much paranormal activity takes place. We decided that we would open up communication over the Board in the room right outside of the laundry room.

Specifically, we were there to make contact with Sharon and Jay, if they were still present, as the owner of the home believed. We opened up the communication and immediately, Jay came through as the main communicator of the group. No sooner than the communication started, a belabored and loud breathing began to my left side. From the communication through the Board, Jay told us, that it was his breathing to let us know that he was present.

Jay told us that they are in this house because the owner of this house experiences them and listens to them. They have a message to be told, which is their truth, the truth about who fathered the baby that was killed when Sharon was murdered. Jay says that he is the father of this baby. The message went like this:

U *[sic]* WILL FIND THERE IS EVIDENCE OF BABY   WHO FATHER IS
POLICE HAVE

I asked Jay if the baby knows who its father is.

Jay said:

BABY KNOWS

Jay further said:

WANTS TO GET THEIR TRUTH OUT   FRUSTRATED   WANT TRUTH
OUT   TRUTH OUT

I asked what happened to the other victims of that horrific murder
scene.

Referring to Abigail, Voyteck and the unborn baby, Jay said:

GONE IN LIGHT LONG AGO

In reference to Steven, another victim of that horrific evening who was
unrelated to Sharon and her friends, Jay said:

YOUNG MAN FEELS CHEATED   LIFE TAKEN   HIS LIFE IMPORTANT
TOO   A TRADGITY *[sic]* FOR ALL THAT DAY

I asked if Sharon had a message to give and Sharon said the following
in reference to Jay:

WE LOVE EACH OTHER   VERY LUCKY HAVE EACH OTHER   THANK
YOU

In the case with this story, the deceased people's spirits became
stuck and earthbound in order to get their messages out and will stay
until they are heard. Although, these messages have been given before
to the owner of this house and there has been speculation in the public
about the baby's father, Jay and Sharon will continue to stay around
until the truth is publically known. Steven stays around because his
story needs to be acknowledged too. All three of them are bound to
this earth by their intense emotions of frustration and anger.
Frustration is what Jay and Sharon feel with the public not knowing
the truth about their love affair and the unborn baby that was theirs.
Anger is what Steven feels for having been at the wrong place at the
wrong time and having his young life of eighteen years taken away
from him so brutally. He wants his life to be acknowledged as having
just as much importance as Sharon and her famous friends' lives had.

As I write this account, I still feel the nausea I felt when I walked
through that lower living area, laundry and storage rooms. My Ouija
Board partner, who assisted me that day, and I both agree that an
experience like this will forever remain etched within our beings, let
alone our psyche.

125

Chapter 7 - Angels, Guides & Ethereal Beings

FIRST STEP BELIEVE YOU DESERVE IT
- Mary Angel

Ethereal beings are what I like to call my spirit friends from the other side. They are actually non-physical beings that exist outside of what we would consider "normal" reality. They are not considered human. Ethereal beings are comprised of pure spirit beings that have never had an incarnation in a physical form and of the celestial world, meaning, what many of us have come to know as Angelic Beings.

I have learned from my work with the Ouija that celestial beings, our angels, can either be comprised of humans who have been elevated into an angelic status or by those angelic beings who have always existed within this celestial force and they too, like ethereal beings, have never had an incarnation in a physical form.

Mary Angel

My Angel, whom I call, Mary Angel, is an angel that was a human before. In her last incarnation, she was a child who died at birth. Such a pure form of love, she was transformed into a celestial being when she passed, as she had completed her evolution with being born into human form. Now, she evolves her soul on the other side, guarding and

126

guiding the people she chooses to watch over. She has always been around me, but it was on May 28, 1994 that she came to me to tell me her name and teach me more about how the angelic realm works.

Ethereal Beings, especially celestial beings, choose to take on any form they feel will be the most well received when they show themselves to humans. In the case of my Mary Angel, she chooses to show herself to me as a female form in her early thirties. They can also appear as animals. In one instance, Mary Angel came to me as a friendly little cat from out of nowhere when I had a flat tire that I was struggling to change. It had been one of those days from hell where everything was a challenge. The little cat came up to me and rubbed up against my legs and body as I was changing the flat. I felt a sense of calm come over me, while feeling wrapped in peace and perfection in that moment. It was the highlight of my day and all of my worries from the day washed away as that cat rubbed up against me. No sooner than the little fellow appeared, I turned around and it was gone and nowhere to be seen. Yet, I was left with peaceful warmth surrounding me.

Guardians or Guides can be of the ethereal and celestial beings or of the deceased humans and animals in spirit form now. My Mary Angel is a guiding angel. I am told that there are many kinds of angels, including guardian and guiding angels. The two ethereal beings I speak with the most frequently now serve as guides, not guardians. Over the years, various deceased humans have been my guardians too. I have experienced guardians and guides having two different distinct roles from each other. The guardians help protect me and engender to keep me from harm's way without interfering with my soul's contract and lessons for this life. I may find myself in predicaments and they intervene when they can without crossing my boundary of free will.

The guides on the other hand, are there to keep me remaining on task with learning the lessons of this incarnation. They lovingly communicate to me through their clues, such as signs, symbols, synchronistic events, a song, a book I may pick up, an animal that crosses my path, a conversation I overheard and license plate messages, to name a few. They work to remind me that I am on path and when I'm not on path, they gently nudge me back by providing their clues. Both the guardians and guides are positioned on the other side to help us awaken to our greatness, to grow and to evolve in our spiritual awareness of our connection to All That Is*. They work to teach us about the importance of learning to live from our hearts and learning to ultimately love ourselves from our hearts. They are basically teachers of love. As they work with us from the other side, they are also growing and evolving as helpers. They have simple rules;

they cannot interfere with our choice of free will, but can intervene with our free will when we ask for their guidance and assistance.

This incredible group of helpers from the other side patiently waits for us to awaken and request their guidance. When I work with the Ouija Board, I am working with a direct connection to them as I directly request their assistance. They wait for these moments and applaud us when we can be open to allow their help. After all, we are here to learn how to be open to experience the love of all forces, the seen and the unseen.

The Sun & the Moon

The Sun and the Moon are names that I have given to my two main spirit guides I communicate with regularly on the Board. They are both of the ethereal realm, meaning they have never been incarnated in physical form. They are of pure spirit energy of All That Is. Every single one of us is a part of this spirit energy as that is the force that flows through us. However, these beings do not have an attachment to anything physical or to an ego-based personality. This means that they are the flow of spirit, which is what we would call love-based feelings. They are complimentary to each other and bring to my experiences a balance of the male and female energy of spirit. Although spirit is truly androgynous, they come in forms for me that I will understand and

129

relate to more readily. Since I work with the blending of opposites within my life's work, my writings and my personal work, it makes sense to me that they represent one energy together, yet comprised of the balance of opposites, the blending of masculinity and femininity, the polarities within. Again, these ethereal and celestial beings will come to each of us in the most relatable form, specific to what you will be able to understand and welcome.

The Sun and the Moon originally entered my life on September 21, 1994. They entered following another ethereal being known as The Big One. The Big One introduced me to the Sun and also let me know that the Sun, the masculine energy, came to me in a dream the night before coming to me on the Board. When the Sun entered the Board, he told me that he would be with me through the rest of my life. The Sun further said,

YOU WERE NOT READY FOR ME UNTIL NOW   THIS LEVEL NOT REACHED OFTEN

He went on to tell me that he really has no name but to use the name that make sense to me and I picked his name from the place where he enters the Board. He comes in at the symbol of the sun on the Ouija Board. Likewise, the Moon comes in at the symbol of the moon and is a feminine influence.

To back track, The Big One was a name I gave it based upon its messages and the energy we felt when it came through the Board. When different entities come through the Board, each one has a different feeling. The way and the side they enter the Board, how they circle or spiral around the Board before communicating, the pressure your fingers feel when the planchette moves and the speed and movement about the Board, signals different entities coming through the portal. After awhile from the experiences of speaking with your various spirits, you begin to know to whom you are speaking via their "fingerprint," if you will, how they move about the Board. This awareness comes after much use and consistency with communication on the Board.

The Big One was also an ethereal being, never incarnated in physical form and here to help others to progress via direct information that was cutting and to the point. Whereas the Sun and Moon, asked questions, much like a yogi would. The questions were to make me and the other session participants look deeper inside for the answers. The Big One encouraged us through statements of information. It was as if during that era, we were receiving a download of information. The Sun and the Moon explained The Big One in the following manner:

IS ALL OF UNIVERSE   WE HELP   HE IS LAST THRU [*sic*] TO LIGHT
THE OTHERSIDE   IN SOME WAYS WERE [*sic*] ALL ONE

The messages came in two very different techniques and styles
and two very different levels of dissemination. In one way, the
message was given to us; the other way encouraged us to dig deeper to
discover the message. Once we got to our communication with the Sun
and Moon, nothing was easy anymore. We now had to be an active
participant and learn to dig deeper within ourselves instead of just
downloading the information.

The Sun and Moon's role on the other side is to serve as "healing
spirits." This means that they are what you and I might call guides or
mediators. They chose to stay and protect and not go into the light to
stay. They are from "God, the Universe" and are of pure light and spirit,
but they stay back from the "typical" process of merging with the light
and work as emissaries (this is my word to describe them.) They used
their free will of choice to stay and help many by escorting them into
the light when they pass over. They tell me that,

NOT EVERYONE HAS THE STRENGTH TO KNOW ITS GOOD TO GO
INTO THE LIGHT   WE HELP THEM GO

They work with me on the level of "friends to help me get the
answers" I seek, so I may too share with the living what they are doing

to help the deceased. They tell me that "someday [they] will help you with the light."

They not only speak to me, but to others who are also in physical form, however, for right now, they are mainly speaking to me. Due to depth and breadth of my inquiries about the intra-workings of the Universe I ask, sometimes their answers come as a need to know basis. They tell me that as we advance in our spiritual understanding and knowledge, we change friends on the other side, which translates to new interactions on the Board. This is not unlike what happens with friends and people we know throughout our lives on the physical plane. We outgrow friends and move on and the same with our spiritual guides and friends. As I progress, they progress, and vice a versa. This means that they are also evolving, as all ethereal beings are growing when we interact with them. Every being in this relationship is expanding in awareness and evolving back to the God source, the Universal consciousness. We help each other do this. This is why it is important to do your work with your often, unseen guides and helpers on the spiritual plane of existence. As we do our work and they do their work, we all are elevated in stature. However, they cannot interfere with our life. They can only intervene if we call upon them and allow. They are thus influenced in their growth by our ability to call upon them and allow them to step in and assist. Save an angel; call upon them!

Other Spirit Guides

Over the years, I have met many different spirit guides from the other side. Each one has a unique name and a unique feeling to them as they move the planchette around the Board to spell. They come forward deemed by the nature of the inquiries and sometimes this equates to a one-time communication with them. Other times, they may continue the contact over multiple sessions or even over multiple decades. I don't concern myself with this as much as I used to. I have learned not to get too attached to any one guide's communication over the Board. Every communication has its purpose and its duration. No different than how we humans evolve through our life lessons, they also evolve through the interactions they have with us on this side and those on the other side. Just when I am becoming comfortable with one spirit guide's manner of communication and their information, they may take a back seat for a while or may even leave all together. However, I do have some favorites with fond memories, such as my communications with Wilma Jean and Mary Angel.

Another interesting component to attracting spirit guides, I have found that depending upon the other person who is operating the

Board with me, we often bring in those guides who are unique to the connection the two of us share. They are attracted to the energy we emit together. Every being has their unique "signature vibration" and when two or more are gathered, the energy changes per the mixing up of the unique energies. Thus, spirit guides are attracted to this newly created frequency that is unique between any given two people. I've experienced a spirit guide who would only come through to communicate when I was operating the Board with the same individual. Once I switched partners, another guide, unique to our experience together would come through. There have been too many different guides with various names to provide them all here, but as I have already shared with you, I discussed a few of them who have been prominent in their interactions with my Ouija Partners and me over the years.

Given this type of interaction between non-physical beings and physical beings, the "feeling of the energy" is what draws them to us. It's the energy of the opened portal, the energy of the Board Operators, the energy of the non-physical being and the energy of the surrounding atmosphere that creates and, ultimately, affects the type and level of communication you will receive through the Board.

Chapter 8 - Consciousness Communication

BELIEVE AND IT IS
- *The Higher Self*

We are conscious beings, although some may beg to differ because of how we go about unconsciously living our lives! Since we humans are created with a consciousness that's part of our DNA makeup, we are made very similar to each other, yet we separate ourselves into different cultures, different nations, different continents that sustain ourselves unconsciously in hate and fear. Instead of acknowledging this fear caused from of our separatism, we engender wars against the other groups in the name of The Great Creator whom all of us share and whose message teaches us to come together in love. We continue to blame our wars on: they did this to us, she took that from us and he threw this at us and so on, all the while, never really waking up to the truth that we are intricately connected to each other. We are adversely and inversely affected by our own actions and then by the others' retaliation, with every stick and stone we throw at their bones.

I bring this up because one of the ultimate lessons that has been a main staple of Ouija communication throughout the years, is the message of the individual's responsibility for her awareness of consciousness within her own life and with others. Time and time again, the message raises its hand to speak and reminds us that we are all connected at the collective consciousness, the underlying universal matrix of spirit, which many call God. We must wake up in our awareness to our interconnectedness. We must finally realize that we might save ourselves the trouble of wasting money and sacrificing human lives with war, which inadvertently, aims those sticks and stones directly at our own bones. It's a boomarang effect. We are ultimately throwing them at ourselves. Our Higher Selves understand the interconnectedness of our collective consciousness.

The Higher Self

There was a period of time during my work with Ouija where we would only speak to our Higher Selves. This was during the years 1989 through 1993 and it involved three of us, Roberta, Mark and me. It was an experiment at first to push the boundaries to whom or with what I thought was possible or impossible to speak. Speaking with the Higher Self is one of the simplest and of course, most direct form of communication with consciousness. After all, it's communication with that part of our self that truly knows our own truths that are kept inside. Then it became a form of communication that made the most sense, as it is bare bones where nothing can escape the light of truth. In other words, you can't hide from yourself.

137

The messages from the Higher Self are very direct and often profound. It feels as if I'm speaking to another ethereal being instead of just me. Actually, the "me" is a spark of the divine matrix of energy, of the God force, so in effect, I am speaking to that pure most conscious part of myself. During this time, I learned that not only would our Higher Selves of others that were involved in the session would communicate with each of us, but a merging of their energies and messages would happen. For instance, my Higher Self didn't just operate alone and speak to me only, it was fortified in its message by the involvement of the other Higher Selves present along with my Higher Self in that room during that session. Envision the notion where the sum is greater than the parts alone. It was as if our Higher Selves' consciousness merged into a group think tank or a hive mind.

Our messages became more profound as we practiced and accepted this merging together of thoughts and awareness. Yet, our messages were still pertinent to our own individual path and our own life and questions, but so profound to the level where all could walk away from the messages and understand it's universal application. The messages were beneficial and fitting for ourselves, yet also applicable to others who were not present. In this next section, I will share some of these profound messages, which are really Higher Self quotes pertinent to spiritual growth and soul evolution to our guiding physical plan, called the human experience.

Higher Self Messages

I have included these messages that came from our Higher Selves during that three and a half year period categorized under specific headings. Although you don't know the context in which these messages were shared, they are timeless and can stand on their own meaning. I present these messages in this book to serve as a reference point to hopefully bring you solace as you work on these concepts within your own life.

Self Love & Heart

KAREN VISIT ME MORE OFTEN   LIKE YOURSELF   THE SELF IS TIMELESS   LOVE YOURSELF LIKE NO OTHER

LOVE HEART WITHIN YOU   SELF LOVE GREATEST LOVE   LOVE IS THE ONLY TRUE HEALER

LIMITS ARE CREATED BY THE MIND   LOVE YOURSELF

FOLLOW YOUR HEART IT WILL LEAD U [*sic*] WHERE U WILL FIND IT
WILL BE THE RIGHT PLACE

CROW PLACE (meaning, "as a crow flies") FIND LOVE AND
UNDERSTANDING   FLIGHT IS FREEDOM NOW   U [*sic*] CAN SOAR   IT
IS A BEGINNING   IT WILL OPEN AND UNLOCK MANY DOORS   SPEAK
BUT ALSO LISTEN WITH AN OPEN HEART FOR GREAT KNWOLEDGE
[*sic*] AND WISDOM COMES FROM THIS   THIS WILL TAKE PRACTICE
FOR THE MIND IS STRONG

Knowledge & Truth

ME AND U [*sic*] HAVE DEEMED IT NECESSARY TO FIND TRUTH
WITHIN

SEARCH FOR TRUTH   SITUATIONS NOT ALWAYS WHAT THEY SEEM

LOOK AND YOU SHALL FIND   WE GO TO TRUTH   MEET LIFE HEAD
ON   DON'T SELL YOURSELF SHORT

KNOWLEDGE IS TRUTH   KNOWLEDGE IS THE WAY SO WE CAN FIND
TRUTH   NO OBSTICAL [*sic*] CANT BE OVERCOME   U [*sic*] HAVE HAD
DOUBTS THAT U HAD TO OVERCOME   THERE WILL ALWAYS BE

SOME BUT U SHOULD NOT JUDGE THAT AS BAD   EDUCATION IN

ANY FORM IS NECESSARY FOR A PERSON TO GROW ON ANY LEVEL

OF EXISTENCE

JOT DOWN WHAT U [*sic*] HEAR   THE TRUTH IS THAT   ALL WE

KNOW IS ALL WE KNOW BUT IS IT ENOUGH   ENOUGH SHOULD BE

WHAT WE KNOW   WE MUST STRIVE FOR MORE KNOWLEDGE BUT

WE SHOULDNT BE DISSATISFIED WITH WHAT WE HAVE LEARNED

GO WITHIN TO KNOW THE TRUTH OF SELF   TRUST SELF AND

NEVER BE DECEIVED

DOES IT MATTER THAT U [*sic*] KNOW WHO IS WHO   LISTEN TO

YOUR INTUTION OR VOICE OR WHATEVER U WANT TO CALL IT

TRUST IN YOURSELF TO DISTINGUISH THE BEST INFORMATION

LOOK INSIDE   BUT WE KNOW THAT ALL KNOWLEDGE CAN BE

FOUND WITHIN   CLEAR YOUR MIND   LOOK TO FIND THE PATH

INSIDE   U [*sic*] ARE THE VEHICLE

LISTEN TO YOUR OWN VOICE NOT TO THOSE WHO WOULD GUIDE

YOU TO THEIR OWN REALITY FOR THEIR OWN SELFISHNESS NO

MATTER HOW KNOBLE THIS MAY BE FOR THEY MEAN WELL BUT
THEY ARE INSECURE BUT HONORABLE NONETHELESS FOR THEY
LOVE YOU

THERE IS IRRITATION THAT WE DO NOT ANSWER   BETTER JUST
CLOSE YOUR EYES AND U [*sic*] CAN FIND ALL THE ANSWERS   GOD
HAS MADE IT THAT WAY

I AM NOT HERE FOR YOU   I AM HERE FOR ALL   VERY FEW ARE
WILLING TO HEAR   EVEN THOSE THAT PROCLAM [*sic*] TO ARE NOT
OF THOSE WHO HONOR THEIR SELF FIND TRUTH IN THIS TYPE OF
WISDOM   THEY HAVE DONE MUCH WORK TO BEGIN THEIR
WISDOM AND RECOGNIZE THEIR OWN PERSONAL TRUTH   THEY DO
NOT HAVE TO ASK FROM WITHOUT

Believe & Know

DECIDE TO HAVE AND YOU WILL   YOU ARE ALL THAT YOU BELEIVE

JUST KNOW THAT YOU CREATE YOUR OWN LIFE SO YOU DECIDE TO
BELIEVE IN U [*sic*]
MAKE YOURSELF THE MASTER OF YOURSELF
1.) REALIZATION

2.) TAKE ACTION

3.) BELIEVE IN WHAT U CAN ACCOMPLISH

4.) DON'T BE AFRAID TO NEED HELP ESPECIALY FROM ME

5.) NEVER GIVE UP

BELIEVE THAT U [*sic*] CAN THEN LET YOURSELF GO TO IT   BE CLEAR IN WHAT U WANT   BE SPECIFIC

The Soul

LOVE SOUL   THE ONLY THING THAT IS ETERNAL   SEE PAST THE MATERIAL   IT WILL ONLY GO AWAY   TRULY IT IS DUST TO DUST LOOK TO THE TRULY IMPORTANT   THE INNER TRUTH   THE SOUL

WHEN YOU ARE AT YOUR MOST INTENSE TRAINING OF MIND IN CONCENTRATION AND CONTEMPLATING YOUR MOST INTERNALNESS AND THOUGHTS   I AM PART OF YOUR SOUL CONSCIOUSNESS

THERE ARE MANY INFLUENCES ON OUR SOULS   EACH INFLUENCES US IN A DIFFERENT WAY   NO KNOWLEDGE IS NEGATIVE   IT IS HOW WE PERCEIVE IT AND HOW WE ACT ON IT

WE ARE ESSENCES OF OUR SOULS   WE KNOW THOSE SOULS BUT
WE WERE NEVER ONE   MANY SOULS CONNECT BUT IT IS A TRUE
GIFT BECAUSE MANY SOULS ARE FOREVER ALONE   WE SOULS ARE
ALWAYS WILL BE ONE NO MATTER WHAT OUR SOULS ARE   ONE
ENTITY ALWAYS   ALWAYS   SOULS ONCE CONNECTED ARE LINKED
EVEN WHEN PHISICAL *[sic]* SEPARATION HAPPENS

Problems are Opportunities

NO PROBLEMS ARE TO *[sic]* GREAT TO DEAL WITH

DO BECOME MORE PATIENT AND REWARDS WILL COME THREE
FOLD

BLOWN OPPORTUNITIES ARE NEVER RETURNED   TO CREATE NEW
OPPORTUNITIES IS A WASTE OF ENERGY SO TAKE ADVANTAGE THE
FIRST TIME

NO ONE CAN MAKE YOU ANGRY   YOU ALLOW YOURSELF TO
BECOME ANGRY

Dreams

DAY LIGHT DOES NOT PUT TO SLEEP THE IMAGINATION   THE DREAMS DURING SLEEP CAN BE JUST AS REAL AS DREAMS WHILE AWAKE   U [*sic*] ARE TRYING TO MAKE EVERYTHING THE SAME FOR U   IT CAN BE THE SAME PLACE BUT FOR OTHERS IT MAY BE DIFFERENT   DREAMS ARE FLIGHTS TO ANY PLACE ONE NEEDS TO GO   ANYTHING IS POSSIBLE IF YOU BELIEVE   DREAMS ALLOW U TO TRAVEL WITHOUT YOUR BODY   U HAVE BODY TO TRAVEL ON THAT PLANE [*sic*]   THAT IS WHY YOU ARE THERE

THE DREAMS DURING SLEEP CAN BE JUST AS REAL AS DREAMS WHILE AWAKE

Talents

THE GREAT JOY OF LIFE IS TO DISCOVER ONES TALENTS REMEMBER TALENTS DO NOT JUST STOP   NEW WILL ARISE MOZART HAD A TALENT BUT HE STRUGGLED WITH IT   WHAT MAKES HIS MORE IMPORTANT THAN SOMEONE WHOM DELIVERS THE NEWSPAPER WELL

Happiness

HAPPINESS LIES IN THE PATH NOT THE DESTINATION   FOR EACH
PATH TAKEN THERE MUST BE AN END EVEN IF IT OCCURS RIGHT
NOW   AS IT ENDS IT DOES NOT STOP   IT CHANGES TO ANOTHER
PATH OR FORM AS U [*sic*] SAID   AS U TRAVEL A LIFE PATH U MAKE
CHOICES   EACH CHOICE LEADS TO ANOTHER SO THIS PROCESS OF
MAKING DECISIONS IS WHERE TRUE HAPPINESS COMES FROM   NOT
ANY ONE RESULT OF A DECISION   RESULTS CAN BRING JOY BUT
ONLY FOR A MOMENT   THE TRAILS LEADING TO THAT MOMENT
ARE HOW ONE DISCOVERS WHAT LIVING IS ALL ABOUT   OPEN US
[*sic*] MIND

HIDE NO MORE   BE HAPPY   ALL TEAMS ARE ONE   WE ARE A TEAM

Change

LIFE HOLDS MANY CHANGES   HOW WELL A PERSON USES THEM IS
THE KEY   CHANGES ARE OPPORTUNITIES FOR GROWTH

CHANGE WILL OCCUR SO BE ABLE TO FLOW WITH IT   BELIEVE IN
YOURSELF   GOOD CHANGE ALWAYS OCCURS

Money

MONEY IS JUST MATERIAL   IT HAS NO FOUNDATION   TOO MUCH
EMPHASIS IS PLACED ON MONATERY [*sic*] GAINS   THAT WILL BE
TAKEN CARE OF   DO NOT PLACE EMPHASIS ON PROFIT FOR PROFIT
BUT ON OWN WORTH   THIS WILL BRING YOU THE WEALTH YOU
SEARCH FOR   IT IS THE PROCESS OF KNOWLEDGE SHARING THAT
MAKES YOU OF WEALTH

Animal Communication

One of the most enlivening forms of communication via the Board
was when we would speak with my pets. Now, I'm not just talking
about speaking to my deceased cats, I am also including in this
category, speaking to my cats when they were/are alive and well.

The first time I stumbled upon this phenomenon was when I was
involved in a session on January 26, 1996 and my very much alive,
orange tabby cat named Hermes interrupted a conversation we were
having with my Angel. Hermes come through after Mary Angel told me
that "YOU ARENT GOING TO BELIEVE THIS" and gave a message to us
over the Board. It came through as a very different energy and we
could tell that something and someone on the other side of the portal
had shifted by the way the planchette moved. The pace of the

planchette slowed down and a sweet message spelled: HERME [*sic*]

CAT I LOVE YOU.

As I continued to explore the concept of animal communication, in one session on February 18, 1996, my spirit friends' message discussed the reason my two cats were in my life, alluding to a lesson they were teaching me about other people:

THE CATS ARE IN YOUR LIFE FOR A REASON   UNCONDITIONALLY THEY CAN DO NO WRONG IN YOUR HEART BECAUSE ACCEPT THEM AS THEY ARE   THEY IS [*sic*] PERFECT   OTHERS ARE THE SAME

Throughout the years I continued to speak to Hermes and also to his companion, the alpha cat of the pair, a tiger striped tabby named, Bill William, after they had both passed on. During these times, I called upon them to come forward and engage in conversation. It's always very touching when a pet comes through and communicates because after all, it's a very similar feeling to communicating with a beloved human that has passed over. It's a moment recaptured in time of all of those feelings we felt: the happiness, sadness and laughter while reminiscing, remembering and still sharing the relationship. The big difference, though, is that you get to see the words in a form you can understand, now, from the beloved pet. I much prefer communicating with my cats while they are still alive than after they pass, but not all of us have had this opportunity. It's definitely an honor and brings such joy.

What I so appreciate about the animal communication whether they are alive or deceased is that they tend to have humor. Maybe it's not so much they have humor in the terms of what we would think of being funny, but it's in the way they just bluntly and simplistically say how things are and were. It sounds funny, I suspect, because they say things with the innocence of a child who just blurts out stories and feelings without a filter. Now, I'm not the only one laughing when these messages come through. All of my fellow Ouija Board Operators are too. The animal messages are so pure, touching and absolutely adorable.

I will say this, our animals greatly appreciate us and express nothing but their authentic selves to us. They continue on into the light when they die and are awaiting our reunion with them. When alive, of course they teach us about unconditional love, dedication, friendship and fun. When we get to see their words spelled out, we see that they fully understand experiencing joy that is only found in the present moment, unlike humans who often hold on to bygones. I'm a believer that all we ever truly need to learn about the heart of what matters, we can learn this from our pets.

Over the years, the spirits have shared with me that animal communication through the Board and through other means happens by matching one's energy frequency with the source one is working to contact. In the instance of communicating with my cats, the spirits shift their energy frequency to match the animal kingdom's frequency. By the way, I am told this is also how the spirits communicate with humans.

The animals don't communicate as frequently over the Board as do the other spirits. This is because the animals tend to not need to communicate with us in this manner and quite frankly, it's a challenging feat for them to communicate in this fashion whether dead or alive. They often find the request silly, as their way of communicating with us is nonverbal and through the feeling centers of our body, specifically, the heart. They feel, we feel and when they are alive, they communicate with us in this manner. So, to ask them to speak with us in a verbal, let alone written manner is over the top. They love us and will try to do so with the help of the spirits' energetic frequency, as stated previously.

On September 15, 2013, I decided to further speak to the spirits, specifically the MOON about animal communication, and then ask the Moon's help to guide a session of conversing with one of my current, alive cats, Panzer, a solid black tabby.

The MOON said:

THEY DO TALK TO YOU EVERYDAY   YOU CAN FEEL IT AND SEE HOW THEY FEEL LOOKING INTO EYES

I then inquired if Panzer would come through and speak with me.

Panzer said:

LOVE YOU   GEART [*sic*] LIVING HERE   LIKE THIS HOUSE

I asked: Which one of our homes do you like the best? (We live in two different homes.)

Panzer said:

HERE (which is our house in the desert) MORE BIRDS TO WATCH

I asked: Remember the time you got out of the house and you were gone for a week and when you finally came home, you had bloody paws and were crying?

Panzer said:

GOT A LITTLE HER   BOY FRIENDS BEAT ME UP

151

I asked: Why did it take you so long to return home?

Panzer said:

WAS IN LOVE

I asked: How could you be in love so quickly?

Panzer said:

SMELLED SO GOOD

I asked: Was Jack (my other cat who is Panzer's half brother) worried when you were gone?

Panzer said:

JEALOUS   HE IS SUCH A PUSSY HIMSELF   WHY DO YOU THINK I GO AFTER HIM   HE NEEDS TO TOUGEN [*sic*] UP[2]

I asked: Why is Jack so afraid?

Panzer said:

LEAVE PAST[3]   HE HAS A GREAT MOM

---

[2] Often Panzer will pin Jack under his legs and grab him by his teeth as the scruff of his neck until Jack meows "uncle!"

I asked: What happened that one night when you knocked a sliding screen to the ground, out of its track and you fought a cat outside to quickly return from the scuffle and end up back in bed?

Panzer said:

STAY OUT OF MY YARD   ITS MINE   HE KNOWS NOW

I asked: Why won't Jack talk to me now?

Panzer said:

LAZY

I asked: How can I help Jack get over being afraid of all visiting houseguests?

Panzer said:

YOU DO   NEEDS TO HELP SELF DUMPASS [*sic*]   SHIT OR GET OFF THE SELF PITY

I asked: Do you still see Bill William and Hermes around? (Deceased cats prior to Panzer and Jack)

---

3 Both cats were rescue cats from a house where a man physically abused them with Jack suffering the brunt of the abuse.

Panzer said:

THEY HAVE MOVED ON

I asked: What can you tell me about Jack's past and what he remembers?

Panzer said:

MOVED ON   HE SHOULD BE HAPPY

I asked: Does he know he's safe now?

Panzer said:

YES   NOTHING HERE WILL HURT HIM

I asked: Do you like the chicken suit I dress you up in?

Panzer said:

NO   IM A VAMPIRE   IT SHOULD BE FOR JACK   HE IS A CHICKEN ARE YOU KIDDING ME

I asked: Then why do you let me dress you up in your hoodies and onesie?[4]

Panzer said:

YOUR [*sic*] THE BOSS

I said: You are a badass cat!

Panzer said:

I AM   LEARNED FROM THE BEST MOM

I asked: Who helps you talk to me?

Panzer said:

I HAVE NO IDEA   ME I GUESS

So, fair is fair and I wanted to hear Jack's side of the story because, after all, he was mocked during the conversation I had with Panzer. I was told then that Jack didn't want to talk on the Board to me, but on September 26, 2013 I inquired again to see if both cats wanted to talk,

---

[4] Panzer will lie on his back calmly and help me place his legs into his outfits.

especially if Jack would. Rhonda and I were talking with the spirit named, Healing Spirit, on the Board when I inquired if it would help us communicate with the cats. The planchette went around in circles on the Board for what seemed like an eternity, while we waited patiently. It felt like we were placed on hold, listening to that irritating office music while Healing Spirit was attempting a three way call with the cats. Finally, Healing Spirit returns to our conversation and said:

NO MESSAGE FROM THE CATS (the planchette paused, then continued spelling) ASK THEM

I then spoke out loud as I would to any of my spirit friends over the Board and ask both Panzer and Jack what they had to say. Nothing. Then, I decided to just speak to Jack and again invite him to speak with me.

I asked: How do feel about your life with me?

Jack said:

ALL GOOD   NO COMPLANTS [*sic*]   GOOD MOM   REALLY THE BEST

I asked: Very curious Jack, what question do you have for me?

Jack said:

CAN I HAVE WET FOOD TONIGHT   LOVE IT

I said: I should have some canned tuna available for you.

Jack said:

TUNAS [*sic*] GOOD   ALL MINE

I said: I'll give you some tuna tonight then.

Trust me, I'm trying not to laugh, but Rhonda and I were both tickled by Jack's answer. You must understand that Jack is not the alpha cat and when it's wet food time, Panzer always approaches the bowl first and eats most of it, leaving only scraps for Jack when he steps away. If I stay present during feeding time, when Panzer is done eating, I will say out loud to Jack, "Jack's-turn" in a singsong-like fashion while adding another scoop of wet food to the bowl, often repeating it until he walks over to the bowl to imbibe.

I asked: Out of all the nicknames[5] I have for you, which one is your favorite to be called?

Jack said:

JACKSTER

I thought that was interesting because I don't call him that very often, maybe every now and then? At that moment it hit me that when I say to him during wet food feeding, "Jack's-turn," it actually sounds a lot like "Jackster." Rhonda told me that when she's heard me say that to him, she too thought I was saying "Jackster."

I asked: So, you like your name because you get wet food?

Jack said:

YES

Now, it was time to get to the bottom of why Panzer would say that Jack is lazy.

I asked: Panzer says you are lazy, are you?

---

[5] I call him a slew of varying names that contain the word Jack, such as, cracker-jack, jack-o-lantern, one-eyed jack, jack of all trades, baby jacks, etc.

Jack said:

YES   BECAUSE I CAN   IM A KING

Jack is truly a scaredy cat. Whenever anyone comes over to my house, he runs and hides and will pretty much hide or stay in the bedroom until the guest has left. I attribute this to the abuse he suffered when living the first three years of his life at another house where both cats were physically abused. Jack suffered the worst, being kicked and thrown and to this day, he freaks out when he hears the sound of shoes coming towards him. I decided to broach this subject with him directly, although I heard what Panzer already told me about this.

I said: What do you remember about you life at your previous home before you came to live with me?

Jack said:

ITS PAST   LEAVE IT THERE

I asked: Well, if it's truly "left" in the past, why are you so scared around people?

I further said: And I'm telling you that you are safe here and no one will ever hurt you again.

Jack said:

JUST VERY CAREFUL   IM A LONER

Changing the subject, I asked: What do you think about the outfits I have Panzer wear from time to time?

Jack said:

HA HA   GLAD ITS HIM NOT ME   THATS WHY HE BEATS ME UP SOMETIMES I GIVE HIM SO MUCH SHIT OVER IT

With that answer, Rhonda and I were belly laughing and high fiving. I was quite amused that he cursed, let alone amazed at his funny clever responses. As we were laughing, from out of the bedroom where he was hiding, in walked Jack. I tell you this because it is not normal for him to do this behavior when I have a guest over, especially if we are laughing loudly and behaving excitedly. Yet, Jack walked right over to us where we were engaging the Ouija session, while seated at the dining table. First, he rubbed up against my chair as I reached down to pet him, then shockingly, he walked over to Rhonda's chair,

160

rubbing himself against it and permitted her to touch him and pet him. The whole time this was going on, we had at least one of our hands on the planchette.

I said: What do you want, Jack?

Jack said:

TUNA

I said: Yes, as soon as we are done talking with you.

Rhonda was petting Jack quite a bit when Jack said:

I LIKE RHONDA

We were amazed by his extraordinary bout of friendliness, which is a rarity for him to express to anyone else but me. We discussed this and continued to pet him. Jack then walked away from the table and sat on the floor a few feet away, looked at us before he did an about face and walked back into the bedroom. The planchette started moving at the same time he did this.

From inside the bedroom, Jack said:

161

DONE

I asked: Jack don't you want some tuna now?

Jack said:

OPEN

Knowing that Jack had been patient enough with the communication, as well as waiting for his glorious tuna, I immediately stood up, left the table and went into the kitchen and opened a new package of wet cat food. No sooner than doing that, Jack came back into the dining room, which is around the corner from the kitchen and his food bowl, and stood there waiting patiently for us to leave the kitchen and let him eat his food in peace. We left the kitchen, but spied from around the corner and watched Jack, while he licked his chops, he walked up to his bowl of wet tuna and salmon and chowed. At about this time, Panzer entered the dining room and started to head towards the kitchen. I intercepted and held him until Jack had ample time to eat as much of the food he wanted. After Jack was satiated with his wet food treat, Panzer was released to eat the remaining. Rhonda and I returned to the Board.

I then asked Panzer while he was still eating: What is your favorite food to eat?

Panzer said:

WET

I said: Well, you are such of a pig, I have to get more food for Jack when you are finally finished and its his turn to eat.

Panzer said:

AND YOUR POINT

We went back and forth about other topics when finally, I said and asked: I am writing about you in my current book. What do you think about that?

Panzer said:

IM A STAR.

Left:
Panzer dressed in his chicken outfit. This is the outfit he believes is better suited for Jack!

Below:
Panzer at his finest! He likens himself to a Vampire.

Chapter 9 - Beyond Messages: Teaching & Lessons

KEEP OPEN ANYTHING IS POSSIBLE
AND BELIEVE ANYTHING IS POSSIBLE
THERES A WHOLE WORLD OUT THERE
- Healing Spirit

Spirits' Teachings & What I Learned

The Sill

What is the "Sill" you ask? Well, I didn't fully understand the meaning of the word Sill until quite some time and teachings had past. The Sill is really a lovely metaphor to understanding the path each of us is on with each turn we take, with each threshold we cross, with each metaphoric doorsill or windowsill we go through. The Sill is that unifying principle within us that supports us in all ways. In the words of the Sun, he explained to us on August 11, 1996:

ITS DOORS WINDOWS ALWAYS OPENING AND CHANGING   IT'S A SIGN   SIGNAL TO KEEP OPEN EVERCHANGING   EACH (Sill) HAS OWN MESSAGE

He further equates the Sill to a path. The concept of the Sill was first introduced to us on August, 11, 1996 when spirit encouraged one of the participants to work with it:

NOW LISTEN WITH YOUR HEART AND PUT YOUR PEN DOWN   DO YOU LOVE ME   DO YOU LOVE YOURSELF   FIRST LOVE SILL   THAT IS PURE LOVE THEN YOU WILL GROW BEYOND THIS PLACE   NOW LISTEN   DO YOU LOVE THE SILL   DONT THINK   FEEL   NO DONT THINK   KNOW   FEEL THE TRUTH NOT THINK WHAT YOUR TRUTH IS   BEYOND KNOW WITH YOUR EGO THE BRAIN   STOP THINKING DONT FEEL WITH YOUR BODY   FEEL WITH THE SILL   ALL YOU AND OTHERS NEED TO FEEL WITH THE SILL

On June 1, 1997, the Sun advised a participant named Joelle about her Sill. He said:

YOUR SOUL IS CALLING OUT BUT YOUR EGO WONT LISTEN ONCE AGAIN   STOP FIGHTING BETWEEN YOUR PARTS   THIS IS ALL SET BEFORE YOU CAME INTO THIS LIFE   YOUR EGO IS FIGHTING YOUR SOULS DIVINE DESIRE   YOUR ANSWERS LIE IN THIS SPACE   SILL

I learned that they are asking us to love and feel from this place within, this place within ourselves that is the hologram of the One Being that Plato taught. It is our connection to our divinity and to our God Source* within. When we learn to feel from this space, we are then

166

feeling from our God Source and widening our connection and ultimately, increasing our channels back to this source.

Heart & Soul

On February, 9, 1997, a message was given to a participant named Colleen. Spirit said:

WHEN A SOUL REJOINS THE HUMAN PLAIN [*sic*] THEY KNOW THE STRUGGLES THEY WILL GO THROUGH INCLUDING PAIN FELT AND CAUSED HOWEVER AS THE SOUL LEARNS IN THIS HUMAN PLAIN [*sic*] THEY DO NOT NEED TO GO THROUGH THE PAIN COL (directed to Colleen, nickname they gave her)   YOU CONTINUE TO SAY THAT YOU WANT TO LEARN ALL YOUR LESSONS IN THIS LIFE   SO YOU ARE LEARNING MORE THAN MOST SOULS DO IN A LIFETIME   YOUR SOUL HAD A BLEED THROUGH TO YOUR EGO THAT IS WHY YOU CONTINUE TO SAY THIS

During another session, on June 1, 1997, the Sun provided a message to Joelle, a session participant. He said about her soul:

EGO IS PLAYING TOO BIG A PART OF YOUR LIFE   BALANCE   HEART IS THE CENTED OF YOUR SOUL   LOOK AT IT THIS WAY   HEAD BRAIN IS THE EGO CONTROL   HEART IS THE SOUL   YOUR FIRST REACTION TO SOMETHING IS FROM SOUL   WHEN YOU PONDER TOO LONG THIS IS YOUR HEAD OR EGO

The concept of lost souls as a major cause for pain within the human experience was broached by the Sun on February 10, 1996. The Sun said:

LOST SOULS YOU HAVE   LOST SIGHT OF THE GOD SOURCE   THEY ENJOY THE PLEASURES OF THEIR EGOS TO [*sic*] MUCH

On February 18, 1996, Spirit further told us where the soul resides. Spirit said:

THE SOUL IS ONE OUSTIDE THIS WORLD   IN THIS WORLD THE SOUL MUST LIVE ALSO AS A DREAM WORLD WHICH HAS NO LIMITS AS THIS WORLD   IF ALL ONLY KNEW WHAT IS COULD BE

I have learned that the soul has spiritual dominion over all parts of ourself, but can only influence us from within the dream state while we are here within the human form. However, it is the Axis Mundi* of our world. It is the center of our center within our being that transcends the material and resides in the immaterial. It is the secret that resides within and without, yet knows our true destiny and plight on the human plane of existence, as well as on the spiritual plane.

Inside

Over the years and throughout many sessions, our spirit friends step forward and tell us the same message in varying ways. They remind us that within, we have the answer to every quandary about

168

ourselves. On June 14, 1994, when Mary Angel was communicating with us, she said the following message to me:

YOU ALREADY HAVE THE ANSWER   LOOK INSIDE   ALL ANSWERS ARE INSIDE   YOU ARE GOOD AT IT   TEACH THEM HOW   I TOLD YOU   YOU HAVE ALL OF THE ANSWERS   LOOK INSIDE AT YOUR PURPOSE   ALWAYS CENTER THEN LOOK INSIDE FOR YOUR ANSWERS   THAT IS WHERE THEY HAVE ALWAYS BEEN   GAP (referring to the place between thoughts) YOU HAVE ALL THE ANSWERS YOU NEED

I have learned the importance of hearing outside messages, but going back within and ultimately, listening to myself. This is why I recommend you maintain a spiritual practice, such as journaling that allows you to reflect upon any teachings while working with the Ouija Board, and for that matter, working with any tool or resource outside of yourself. From the late, great poet Robert Frost, comes this eloquent poem that sheds light upon this concept:

> *We dance round in a ring and suppose,*
> *But the Secret sits in the middle and knows.*

Limitations

Ouija Spirits often speak about how we set limitations within our lives, which keep us from expressing our greatness and living our life's path of joy. On February 8, 1996, Spirit spoke to us about the relationship between worry and creating limits. Spirit said:

THE WORLD HAS NO LIMITS   WORRY SETS LIMITS   THE TRICK IS TO KNOW NO LIMITS THUS THIS TYPE OF ENERGY (lack of limits) WILL FLOW TOWARDS YOU 10 FOLD

During a conversation on March 10, 1996, Mary Angel told us about the limitations they have communicating through Ouija. She further said:

MOVING BEYOND THIS OUIJAS LIMITS   FEELINGS (needed) NOT WORDS

I have learned throughout the years, from all of my conversations and messages about limitations that limitations are created by the ego and have no real place within our lives. When we return to spirit form, we will understand that our limiations were illusions. We do not need to ever limit ourselves.

Change

It seems that the entire purpose of using the Ouija Board in my view is to affect change within myself and others. Change is the only constant we have in life. Therefore, count on it! Change is what takes us to new levels of experience and allows us to grow and evolve. Learning that there are not limits, but the limits I impose upon myself, frees my energy to explore the unseen frontiers. Over the years, as I been involved within every single Ouija Session I write about within this book, I have learned that what people fear most is change. If we can see change as an opportunity to bring us into our Greater Self that no matter what happens during the change, the change will bring us into the aspiring promise of who we are meant to be. In a session on July 24, 2013, the session participant, Bev, was reminded the following by the spirits:

REMEMBER YOU CAN ONLY CHANGE YOURSELF   WE ALL NEED TO LOOK AT OURSELF AND WHAT DO I NEED TO WORK ON

Change is a personal task. We can't change others, but we can sure enough change ourselves and that might make all the difference we desire within our worlds.

Money

On June 14, 1994, The Big One entered the Board to speak with me personally about money. The Big One said:

MONEY IS NOT THE ISSUE   LEARN   MONEY WILL COME WHEN YOU NEED IT FOR YOU 2   IT WILL   DONT WORRY ABOUT MONEY   IT WILL FLOW TO YOU IN LARGE AMOUNTS   LET GO OF THE FEAR OF NOT HAVING MONEY

I have learned quite frankly, that we need to get of our own way and let go of money as being the cause for a deeper-seated issue. Typically the fear of money, which does create the literal lack of money, stems from our own sense of unworthiness. For example, on May 14, 1995, Rasja, the Higher Self of Colleen, a participant in the session, came forth and reminded all us present about a powerful teaching of money. Rasja said to Colleen:

THE MONEY IS NEVER GOING TO BE A PROBLEM FOR YOU   LET IT GO   MONEY IS ENERGY   IT SHOULD BE EXCHANGED   YOU ARE WORTH WHAT YOU BELIEVE   YOURE WORTH MORE AND YOU WILL ATTRACT THOSE LIKE YOU   YOU WILL ALWAYS BE PROVIDED FOR

We were also told by Mary Angel on June 22, 1996 how our self worth should not be measured by money. She said:

YOUR WORTH IS NOT MEASURED IN THE MONEY YOU ARE CURRENTLY EARNING

Viewing money as energy that flows and exchanges is an invaluable lesson to understand. I have learned it's a way to honor the ebb and flow of our own finances as they shift and change. By not worrying, not holding onto, but allowing this ebb and flow of energy, we allow the cyclical return of it within our lives. On December 31, 1996, Spirit spoke to us about this concept. Spirit said:

MONEY WILL CONTINUE TO BE LOST IN YOUR LIFE UNTIL YOU
LEARN TO LET THE ENERGY FLOW   REMEMBER IT IS ONLY ENERGY
AND TO BE MOVED AROUND

On July 30, 1997, the Sun continued the conversation about money
viewed as energy. The Sun said:

MONEY IS ENERGY   IT MUST FLOW   YOU ARE NEVER WITHOUT IT
OTHERS NEED YOUR ENERGY (my money) RIGHT NOW   IT WILL
COME BACK TO YOU 10 FOLD   WATCH IT HAPPEN   WE ARE RIGHT

The most important lesson I have learned about money that I
would like to share with you, is the following: money truly is energy
that flows to where it is most needed. As long as we don't step in to
block the flow, it will always flow back to you. The most truly amazing
thing about money that I can personally attest to is this: First and
foremost, let go of its loss or lack within your life and rest assured that
you are always wealthy in many ways. Secondly, come to know
yourself as being worthy of great rewards. Then last but not least,
allow its flow, which is often cyclical in nature, while trusting in a
boundless and abundant source that always provides. Money, like
water, flows in a path of least resistance. Know and allow. I have
learned this is the key to true wealth consciousness.

Flow

The concept of flow the spirits spoke of often seemed like a nebulous, intangible concept to grasp. Actually it is! As I have learned, when we are flowing, we are allowing a faith or a trust in the path or process to emerge. We are working alongside the process, while not capturing the process or trying to control or rush the outcome we want or anticipate. This can be a tough and painful lesson to learn, and this I know. On September 15, 1996, Spirit spoke directly to me and said:

TO TEACH YOU NOT TO WORRY SO MUCH ABOUT DETAILS AND TO LET YOUR LIFE UNFOLD AS THE FLOW MOVES YOU   NOT TO PREDICT THE OUTCOME OR TO CONTROL THE OUTCOME   YOU CREATE WHEN GIVE INTO THE FLOW AND TRUST AND DONT TRY TO CONTROL   TRUST THE FLOW AND ENJOY THE RIDE AND THE VIEW

The lesson of flow was a constant lesson that I would hear during the year 1996. On September 23, 1996, Spirit said to me:

KAREN TAKE LIFE WITH LOVE FIRST AND FORMOST [*sic*]   YOU NEED TO TAKE THINGS LESS SEROUIS [*sic*]   YOU GET TO WOUND UP ABOUT THINGS MEANING YOU ARE NOT FLOWING   YOU ARE FIGHTING THE CURRENT

On October 6, 1996, along came yet another message about flow directed again, to yours truly. Spirit said:

ONLY 1 WORD HOLDS ALL YOU NEED TO KNOW ABOUT WHAT IS
GOING ON IN YOUR LIFE RIGHT NOW KAREN   THE WORD IS
DETACHMENT FROM OUTCOME   KNOW   FEEL   FLOW IS RIGHT

Dreams

I have learned that the dream state is where the spirits of the
deceased and of the ethereal and celestial realms can more readily
visit us, assist us and speak to us. The spirits have told us over and
over again to be open to their connection within our dreams. Many
times we were told to be prepared with paper and pen, ready to go, on
our nightstands. To this day, the spirits come to me within my dreams
and teach me within that realm. Since I have been working with my
dreams, as long as I have been using the Ouija Board, this process
comes naturally to me. Remember, it is within the dream state where
our souls reside while we are in the human form. On February 15,
1996, an ethereal guide by the name of Starm spoke to us about
dreams. Starm said:

DREAM HOLDS ALL THE TRUTHS IN THE UNIVERSE   IN DREAMS
YOU ARE IN TOUCH WITH YOUR SOUL IF YOU CAN GET BEYOND
YOUR EGO BARRIERS

More recently on September 26, 2013, Healing Spirit spoke to me
about it being much easier for them to communicate with me through

my dreams, so I tend to receive much more of my communication with my spirit friends through my dreams now. While speaking with Healing Spirit on the Board, I told him that I have been very aware of their presence and their messages. Healing Spirit said:

WE ARE HERE BECAUSE YOUR [*sic*] OPEN TO THE SPIRITS   TOLD YOU LAST SESSION WE WOULD COME TO YOU IN DREAMS   WE HAVE BEEN TALKING TO YOU

I have learned that dreams are not only representational and reflective of our personal lives. We do not only have dreams to mechanistically work through pressing issues within our lives, but most importantly have dreams to serve as a portal back to our souls and into the spiritual realm from whence we came. We can go on many journeys through our dream state into other realities. We can interact with our deceased loved ones, including our pets. We can travel to far away places and meet beings who impart spiritual knowledge and truths. Within the dream realm, there is more than meets the eye and dwells within our souls.

And with all of these teachings comes a time when you come to the realization, no matter how tough the lessons can be or have been, once you have cross that threshold, the Sill, of a new discovery, you can't go backwards. And truth be known, even if you could, you do not want to anyways.

What Others Learned

While I was writing this book, I reached out to several of the people who have been a part of my Ouija Board experiences over the years, spanning back to 1989 through the present. I simply asked them to share with you what they experienced from participating within a Ouija session with me and consequently, what they have learned as a result. Some have worked the planchette with me and some attended the session as a participant only, while some have particpated in both capacities. I found that no matter what role they participated within a session, the messages and teachings were just as powerful. This goes to show that not everyone must lay their hands on the planchette to benefit from the work. In fact, when the messages are clear, everyone in the room will take something positive away with them.

Chris G.

It was probably around 1985 when I was in college and living in a sorority house that I had my first experience with the Ouija Board with Karen Dahlman. Karen and I were sorority sisters and friends. We enjoyed all the usual college pranks and fun to be had during college life, including experimenting with the Ouija, as we were adventurers!

Karen and I and probably half a dozen other friends used the Ouija on quite a few occasions, but one incident in particular will forever be a part of my memory. Why? This time, I knew it was real. I really knew that it wasn't a parlor trick; the spirits could actually communicate through this tool called the Ouija. How did I know that? First off, only Karen and another friend, Linda, had their hands on the planchette while both of them were blindfolded. This was at the request of a couple of friends who were devout Catholics and definitely were skeptical.

That planchette literally flew around that Board, pointing to letters, rapid-fire as our friend, Dena, diligently wrote each letter down on a piece of paper as fast as she possibly could. None of us present knew the message until Dena read the message after the planchette stopped moving. As Dena read the message, I noticed tears streaming down Lindsey's cheeks; we all wondered who the "Kelly" the message referred to was. Turns out Lindsey had a sister named "Kelly" who had died, and none of us knew other than Linda, who was also wearing a blindfold while touching the planchette. Lindsey, who simply was a witness at the session and never expected that this was coming, was the recipient of a beautiful message from her sister beyond the grave. The rest of us were simply tools and witnesses.

I believe we were all profoundly changed by that experience. For me, it confirmed that there are many aspects of spirituality that are WAY beyond what my Catholic upbringing had taught me. And I wanted to know more. That experience opened my eyes and removed the fear of exploring my own spirituality, on my own terms and outside the "rules," and I continue to explore my spirituality to this day and will continue for the rest of my life.

Of course I picked this instance to share. It was the one that had the most profound effect on me and definitely opened my eyes that there was much more to the spiritual world than I had ever experienced before. Definitely a life changing moment.

Thanks Karen, for exposing me to the Ouija, and teaching me that taking risks allows me to be and experience more than I ever thought possible! Keep teaching people that the Ouija is an effective spiritual tool!

Brian B.

It was late at night during a very intense thunderstorm when I was visitng my then girlfriend, Dena and Karen Dahlman at the apartment the two of them shared.

I had always felt badly for not attending my grandfather's funeral in Utah. We contacted my grandfather and he told me he understood and never gave it a second thought and that he loved and missed me. That night taught me to never forget to keep an open mind and it taught me about tolerance. What an eye-opener. I'm a believer.

Roberta L.

I had my first experience with the Ouija Board when I was in my adolescence and messing around with it to scare ourselves at sleep-overs. Many years later, in 1989, I wast reintroduced to the Ouija Board by Karen Dahlman, but this time as a tool not to be played with or taken lightly, but used to gain knowledge. We approached it seriously to gain insight.

When I look back on those times, I can tell you that there was a big difference in the feel of the information we received and the way the energy flowed. Placing my hands on the Ouija in 1989 compared with curiously playing with the Ouija as a young girl of 12, was an entirely different experience.

Once Karen and I centered and grounded for a Ouija session, this stream of knowledge would just flow. There was none of that erratic movement going all over the place in gibberish that I received as a child. Instead, it flowed in coherent threads. The flow would slow and stop and hover when it did not understand what we were asking or when it was trying to put it's message into the right wording, but it still flowed.

Some people could say, "Well, yeah, that was you driving it or Karen driving it," but it flowed too fluidly and I would argue that surely if it was one or both of us, we would both be vying for the driver's seat. I am convinced that it was our Higher Selves tapping into and connecting into the ethereal realm, working in unison to bring us this stream of knowledge.

One of the most important things Karen brought to the table, was integrity and trust and that is so important when opening yourself up to receiving that which is unknown. In the case of the Ouija Board, you become a conduit, a channel, for this stream of knowledge that is available to everyone. The Ouija is just one way to connect to this information, but remember, like all information, it is subject to interpretation. The information we receive is only as good as the tools we are using and that is why it is so important to make sure the person you are working with is coming from a place of integrity and that you trust them.

Rhonda W.

Using Ouija has helped me in the most amazing ways! I have also seen it help others through the messages they received from deceased loved ones and their guides. I've learned to take the messages that I've received in a session and incorporate them back into my life. For example, I have received a lot of messages about learning to trust myself, my intuition and that it's okay to set boundaries with people in my life who are less than kind to me. Ouija can become a portal to learning life's lessons and I like the way it has uplifted my spirit while learning my lessons. Let's just say that I have learned to find my voice with the help of the spirit friends.

Elise S.

Ouija changed my life! If I would have known that is was going to be such a positive, mind-blowing experience, I would have done it sooner. (Even though I was taught as a Catholic that is was the BAD, BAD Devil and that I would go to hell if I tried it.) I felt so comfortable with Karen, my friend, because I trusted and respected her. As we sat down at the dining room table with the Board, I was a tiny bit nervous but thrilled with anticipation and curiosity. As we called the spirits to the Board, I quickly became acutely aware, awakened and alive. Then I felt this incredible power move through me from the floor into my feet, slowly moving up through the rest of my body, filling my body with warmth and love. The goosebumps tickled me as they grew bigger and bigger. At that moment, I knew my life had changed forever. I was hooked. I can still feel the emotions I felt that day as I write about this experience. (I even have chills right now as I retell this.)

Suddenly, I could feel someone's presence on the Board. I have to admit the fear factor was definitely there! Then this powerful, precise energy moved the planchette that our fingers were touching across the Board, spelling out a code 143 WOMAN J[6]. Get this, there is only one other person in my life who knew what 143 meant and that was my dear friend, Jim, who many years earlier had died practically in my arms at the hospital. He was always precise in his actions and words so his energy on the Board comforted me. No doubt, I immediately knew it was him.

At that moment, I nearly fell off my chair when he wrote "our code" on the Ouija Board. It gets better, though. I've always felt as if he's been guiding me since his death, so when he confirmed for me over the Board and from the Great Beyond that he helped find my Mother a

---

[6] The code "143" was a code specific to two people only, and that was to Elise and Jim. They only spoke that code to each other and to no others. I (Karen) had no idea what this message meant when it came through, let alone did I realize it was a complete, coherent message. Elise explained to me that 143 stood for how many letter are in each word of the code, three words total. It stands for I(1) love(4) you(3), thus I love you: 143!

183

room at an assisted living facility, I knew this to be the truth because my Mother's room number is 143. Recalling back to that day when they assigned my mother the last room available, I looked at the number on her door and it was none other than, 143! Although, I already knew at that moment, my friend Jim was instrumental from the other side, making that happen, it was reaffirming to receive that confirmation on the Board that day.

After this, my curiosity grew. While I knew his spirit was still on the Board, I asked him if he helped me find my husband. He responded "Yes." I knew it, because I felt it at that time, too. After I met my husband, I looked up in the sky, closed my eyes and said, 'Thank you Jim."

Through the Board, I have also met my Angel, who happens to be a female energy named Bonaky. She had amazing energy when she came onto the Board. I remember my hand feeling as if it was taken over by something larger than me and the planchette was moving faster and faster in the figure eight, known as the symbol of infinity. This experience brought the biggest smile to my face and my heart race with excitement. How many people can say they met their angel?

I have learned that life and love do continue on; life after death does exist. It's absolutely a beautiful and secure feeling. I have learned that I am guided and supported by so many loving spirits. Learning this is incredibly moving and emotional for me. I feel safe. I feel secure. I feel love. After my Ouija Board experiences, I learned not to be afraid. Seriously, I used to be afraid of the dark, but not anymore.

You must encounter this for yourself. Don't wait too long. You are going to love it. All of your subconscious questions about important people in your life who past away, will come forth and tell you things NOBODY else would know, but you. This alone, will make you a believer. It's extremely fascinating. You can't lose. It's a win win. You have to try it. Be careful, though, you may become more empowered than you ever have before!

Victoria V.

When I was a young girl at the age of 13, I remember doing OUIJA with a friend, not taking it too seriously, but more as a mysterious game of the "unknown." Now as a woman of 58, experiencing OUIJA has a "Spiritual" quality to it within the context that Karen provides. The questions are answered simply and are pure, like the purity we felt when we were children. The answers are direct and ALWAYS felt at the heart. I've learned that love is the intent to all. OUIJA is a tool or portal to help me journey back to SOURCE. Through the questions I have asked and the responses I have received, the process helps me realign my SOUL on the path of a relationship with the SOURCE , which teaches Universal Love.

Bev M.

It had been literally decades since I had a connection with the Great Beyond through the astounding Ouija Board. Since the death of my father, there has been a tremendous void that I had been experiencing. Following the night's connection via Karen and the Board, I felt I was able to fill it somehow. His words were there, his spirit enveloped the room, and I felt an astounding sense of peace and well-being. I had suspected that Dad was in "a better place," where he didn't experience the disappointments that so many in his life had bestowed upon him. He was a true and kind "giver," and unfortunately received very little in return, as generous nature is many times taken advantage of. My communication with him via Karen's words, assured me that he was continuing to help others, but now, was nurtured by the important people he was able to reunite with following his departure from this world.

The experience with Karen, and a good friend who was also in attendance and lending her support, was invaluable to me. It has helped me evaluate so many facets of my life and assess which road is the right one to journey upon as I stand at a crossroad point with career, life and love. Karen was an incredible "messenger" as the words flowed from my father, a man now enriched with love, peace and total understanding from those he knew from before, and from those he has met along his eternal journey. I will look forward to perhaps reaching my sister, also named Karen, and find out if she has found the peace she fought to experience while on this earth.

It is a life-changing experience to sit with Karen Dahlman and discover an inner peace, inner strength and empowerment through the revelation that "things are ok - will be ok - no matter what." As a chronic worrier, what sense of peace I found that evening, to take with me and carry through each day. Thank you, Karen!

Glossary

All That Is – every single thing is a part of the divine essence, comprising the eternal Universe. It is all of creation.

Axus Mundi – the symbolic, connective element between the immaterial and the material, linking the heavens with humans.

Celestial – the spiritual realm belonging to the angelic beings.

Divination tool – a systematic method that employs a tool or a practice to gain insight.

Esoteric – secret teachings understood by a few.

Ethereal – the spiritual realm belonging to incorporeal spirits, who have never been in physical form.

God Source – the omnipotent Universal source from which all of creation came.

Great Beyond - encompassing all of the unseen realms beyond our senses.

Greater Self – the potential within a human.

Higher Self – the voice of our soul.

Institute of HeartMath® - a nonprofit research and educational organization located in Boulder Creek, CA. Their focus is on employing the guidance of the heart for personal development to create health on all levels. Learn more: heartmath.com.

Karmic contract – the agreement we have with another soul, in place for the purpose of our soul's evolution. Each contract is specific to each relationship.

Sciomancy – practice of speaking with ghosts or spirits for divination purposes.

Soul – the individualized hologram of the divine essence.

Spirit – the breath of life, the energy of the Universe.

Theurgy – practice of invoking spirits for the purpose of personal evolution to unite with the divine source.

Bibliography

Besant, Annie. *Esoteric Christianity or the Lesser Mysteries*. Adamant
   Media Corporation, 2001. Print.

Bond, Elijah J. Ouija or Egyptian Luck-board. Charles W. Kennard and
   William H. A. Maupin, assignee. Patent 446,054. 10 Feb. 1891.
   Print.

Braude, Ann. *Radical Spirits: Spiritualism and Women's Rights in
   Nineteenth-century America*. Bloomington: Indiana UP, 2001.
   Print.

Brown, Slater. *The Heyday of Spiritualism*. New York: Hawthorn, 1970.
   Print.

Casey, Bradley J., Sarah Getz, and Adriana Galvan. "The Adolescent
   Brain." *Developmental Review* 28.1 (2008): 62-77. Print.

Conradt, Stacy. "The Quick 10: 10 Famous Uses of the Ouija Board."
   Mental Floss. Mental Floss, Inc., 21 Oct. 2010. Web. 24 Aug.
   2013. <http://mentalfloss.com/article/26158/quick-10-10-
   famous-uses-ouija-board>.

Doyle, Arthur C. *The History of Spiritualism Vol I*. Arthur Conan Doyle,
   1926. Print.

Hanegraaff, Wouter J., Antoine Faivre, Roelof Van Den Broek, and Jean-
   Pierre Brach. *Dictionary of Gnosis and Western Esotericism*.
   Leiden [u.a.]: Brill, 2005. Print.

Horowitz, Mitch. "Mitch Horowitz - Ouija: A History." *Mitch Horowitz -
Ouija: A History*. Mitch Horowitz, n.d. Web. 15 Sept. 2013.
<http://www.mitchhorowitz.com/ouija.html>.

Horowitz, Mitch. "Spellbound: How the American Anomoly of Ouija
Has Impacted National Life-and Art-over the past Century,."
Esopus 7.Fall (2006): 132-39. *ESOPUS Magazine*. Esopus
Magazine. Web. 15 Sept. 2013.
<http://www.esopusmag.com/contents/view/152>.

Krik, Phyllis. *Quantum Lite: How to Calm the Chaos*. Amazon Digital
Services, 2011. Print.

Livergood, Norman D. "Esoteric Christianity." *The New Enlightenment*.
Norman D. Livergood, 2013. Web. 06 June 2013.
<http://www.hermes-press.com/esoteric_christianity.htm>.

McCraty, Rollin, Mike Atkinson, and Dana Tomasino, Comps. *Science of
the Heart: Exploring the Role of the Heart in Human
Performance*. 001st Ed. Vol. 01. Boulder Creek: HeartMath
Research Center, Institute of HeartMath, 2001. Print.

Murch, Robert L., Jr. "The Story of American's Most Unique Inventor."
*WilliamFuld.com - The Official Website of William Fuld and
Home of the Ouija Board!* Robert L. Murch, Dec. 2007. Web. 7
Sept. 2013. <http://www.williamfuld.com/>.

Nelstrop, Louise, Kevin J. Magill, and Bradley B. Onishi. *Christian*

Mysticism: An Introduction to Contemporary Theoretical Approaches. Farnham, Surrey, England: Ashgate Pub., 2009. 109-10. Print.

"The New 'Planchette.' A Mysterious Talking Board and Table Over Which Northern Ohio Is Agitated." *New York Daily Tribune* 28 Mar. 1886: 9. *WilliamFuld.com - The Official Website of William Fuld and Home of the Ouija Board!* Robert L. Murch, Dec. 2007. Web. 14 Sept. 2013. <http://www.williamfuld.com/ouija_articles_03281886.html>.

Orlando, Eugene. "Ancient Ouija Boards: Fact of Fiction." *Museum of Talking Boards: An Online Museum of Ouija Boards.* Eugene Orlando, 1996. Web. 15 Sept. 2013. <http://www.museumoftalkingboards.com/ancient.html>.

Orlando, Eugene. "History of the Talking Board." *Museum of Talking Boards: An Online Museum of Ouija Boards.* Eugene Orlando, 1996. Web. 14 Sept. 2013. <http://www.museumoftalkingboards.com/history.html>.

"'The Ouija' The Wonder of the Nineteenth Century." *Baltimore Sun* 6 Dec. 1890: n. pag. *Museum of Talking Boards.* Eugene Orlando, 1996. Web. 7 July 2013. <http://www.museumoftalkingboards.com/history.html>.

Palmer, John. "A Mail Survey OF Ouija Board Users in North America."
Free Online Library. Farlex, Inc, 1 Sept. 1999. Web. 29 June
2013. <http://www.thefreelibrary.com/A MAIL SURVEY OF
OUIJA BOARD USERS IN NORTH AMERICA.-a060054207>.

Pedersen, S. "Personality Formation in Adolescence and Its Impact
upon the Psycho-analytical Treatment of Adults." *The
International Journal of Psychoanalysis* 42 (1961): 381-88.
Print.

Zerner, Amy, and Monte Farber. *The Ghost Writer Spirit Guidebook*.
New York: Sterling Co, 2008. Print.

About the Author

Karen A. Dahlman believes that life is meant to be a joyful experience, driven by the expression of our creative inner potentials. She believes that we are able to tap this great source within when we open ourselves to all possibilities.

Within this book, *The Spirits of Ouija – four decades of communication*, she shares all of the insights she gained, while opening up her communication with conscious beings from the Great Beyond via the Ouija Board.

Karen has a strong spiritual connection to her spirit friends as she has throughout her entire life. Highly experienced as a Ouija-ologist (one who studies the uses of the board), she teaches others about the positive benefits of using this tool as a means for expanding and deepening one's world and expression within it in the most profound ways.

Karen's background is as diversified as her writings are controversial. She began her career as a licensed and board certified art therapist, hypnotherapist and counselor after graduating from the University of New Mexico with both her bachelor and master degrees.

For over a decade Karen worked within multiple settings, with varying populations, including her private practice and public workshops, while providing creative and expressive means for her clients to find health.

After spending her formative years living all over the United States, she made Southern California her home in 1999. At that time, Karen hung up her therapy shingle and entered the high-tech industry of telecommunications and founded CVC, Inc., a consulting and utility design firm for the fortune 100 wireless carriers. Coming upon its thirteenth year in operation, Karen remains at the helm as CEO.

Coming full circle within her career, from right brain to left brain to center brain, she strives to maintain a balance of her total brain within her heart. Karen shares within her books, her process of doing this with herself and with others. She endeavors to help others deepen into their unique possibilities to discover their own empowerment to affect personal growth, their spiritual evolution, and a passionate expression of their calling.

Previous Work

The Spirits of Creativity: Embodying Your Soul's Passion
Published 2012

Author Contact

PO Box 1496
San Clemente, CA 92674
karen@creativevisionspublications.com

Made in the USA
Columbia, SC
02 November 2020

23865188R00113